THE CHURCH MILITANT

WAR PRINCIPLES FOR CHURCH LEADERS

DR. CHARLES VOGAN

Copyright © 2010 Charles R Vogan Jr

All Rights Reserved

Scripture taken from the HOLY BIBLE, NEW INTERNATIONAL VERSION, Copyright © 1973, 1978, 1984 International Bible Society. Used by permission of Zondervan Bible Publishers.

ISBN 978-1-928565-99-4

Cover design by Alex Park

Ravenbrook Publishers

A subsidiary of
Shenandoah Bible Ministries

www.shenbible.org

CONTENTS

Introduction	5
The Bible and War	19
Self-Preparation	49
Assessment of the Position	79
Assuming Command	109
Preparation and Planning	149
War Principles	187
Transfer of Command	239
Evaluation	251
Postscript	269
Outline	271
Wesley's Account of his Assemblies	281
Further Resources	287

"In the sphere of Venus I learned war."

C. S. Lewis, *That Hideous Strength*

INTRODUCTION

Praise be to the LORD my Rock, who trains my hands for war, my fingers for battle. (Psalm 144:1)

INTRODUCTION

War is an ugly business. The dilemma of war is this: we want peace, but others are forcing us to fight for what belongs to us; they want it instead. And because they won't take no for an answer, because they send their army to take away what we have, we have to raise an army to fight against them and defend ourselves. Unfortunately, some are going to die as a result.

The Church is in a similar situation. We are surrounded by desperate enemies who want to destroy our peace, undermine our Bible, drain our resources, steal our people away to their side and prevent others from joining us, and generally wreak havoc in our ranks and bring our name into disrepute. And being the good Christians that we are, we are hoping that these enemies will just eventually go away. The problem is that a lot of people are going to suffer and die while we are waiting.

If the church hopes to win its battles in our modern culture, it's time to turn to the tried-and-true principles of war. In fact, the reason we are doing so badly is because, for the most part, church leaders and members refuse to go to a war footing and train for battle (that is, when they are not fighting each other!). As a result, the enemy is tearing the church apart and meeting almost no resistance from us; and we certainly aren't having much influence on our culture anymore.

We *are* in a war, however, and there are real casualties! People are dying every day from the ravages of sin and the forces of darkness. If today's church is in a state of chaos and confusion, it's because its leaders aren't able to switch to war mode and win some of these battles that we are fighting against the Enemy. In contrast, Christians in other ages seemed able to successfully handle the issues that we are failing at so badly.

Introduction

The Bible and war

It may seem strange to apply war strategy to the context of the church, but actually much of the Bible encourages us to do so. The Old Testament, for example, is a record of the people of God battling against the forces of evil in the world: sometimes they won, and many times they lost. Israel's leaders didn't always know the principles of fighting this kind of spiritual war. Moses and David did, but many of the Kings of Judah and Israel failed the nation because of their own sin or from ignorance of God's ways. This was in spite of the fact that the Lord wanted them to learn war, and left undefeated enemies around them.

> He did this only to teach warfare to the descendants of the Israelites who had not had previous battle experience. (Judges 3:2)

The New Testament clearly shows us the Lord Jesus leading his forces against his enemies; the book of Revelation actually paints the picture for us (in chapter 19). But again, church leaders aren't always alert to this Biblical insight, and they aren't able to recognize the battlefield for what it is; they therefore often fail the church as incompetent commanders. Few churches are a military success, spiritually speaking.

Our enemies are not the sort you might think; though we relish a fight with other people, they are enemies only because they are dupes of the real enemies of the Church. The Bible gives three main enemies that can hurt the work of the Church: the *world*, the *flesh*, and the *devil*. Jesus specifically targeted these three scourges in his ministry, and he has given us the mandate and the resources to continue this fight. So we can expect (though most of the principles of the military art and science are common to all warfare) that the military training in the Bible will be specially designed to target these particular foes.

Basic principles – and being alert

In order to train the troops, instill discipline, motivation and passion, and lead the church to victory, the leader has to be able to understand any situation very clearly – and quickly. A military training

Introduction

will teach him what to look for, and how to deal with many kinds of circumstances, in order to achieve success. It's a combination of education and savvy (which in military terminology is called *coup d'oeil*) – the ability to take what you have learned in class and apply it to a particular situation.

There is no secret mystery to the art of war. It's a matter of looking at everything, down to the details; it's a process of breaking down a complex problem into its simple parts and applying tried-and-true principles. But it also involves a great deal of study, thought and prayer. Since the Bible has the answers for all the problems and challenges that the church may face, only the leader who can learn the fundamental principles of *spiritual* warfare (as the Bible describes them), and who applies them rigorously and thoroughly, can hope to win the battle. We will lose battles only if we refuse to obey the Commander's clear instructions; he has provided help for every contingency in his Word.

The leader will also discover that he can't afford to hang back at the edge of battle as the troops often do, and wish that someone else would do the work. He has to be constantly studying; he is always planning and changing the plan to fit the changing circumstances. As Napoleon once said, the commander never sleeps! He is the brain of the outfit, and the troops are his arms and legs. The soldier on the front line fights with his weapon; the leader fights with his men. It's up to you, the leader, to lead the church against the Enemy effectively. So you need to be constantly alert, always planning, and continually leading.

The need for war

Of course you could simply ignore all this emphasis on preparation and training, choosing instead to quietly teach and pastor people; some gentle-hearted leaders don't like all this talk about war. The problem is that something *will* eventually happen that you won't be able to handle because you didn't prepare for it. In other words, you won't be ready or capable of meeting many critical needs of the church. This is a harsh and unforgiving world that we live in.

Introduction

- Someone will oppose you and try to destroy your work.

- Someone is going to need something that you can't give them.

- You will be missing critical elements in your ministry that will prevent you from achieving the Mission that the Lord gave you.

- You won't be ready for unexpected trials or circumstances.

Human nature being what it is, and since this world is so broken, don't naively think that your ministry will be without troubles or problems. You simply have to prepare for these situations *before* they happen if you want to be an effective leader. The only other responsible action is to quit the ministry so that you don't lead your church members into a disaster.

If you have ever listened to a group of pastors talking, you will hear this line over and over: "I wish I knew then what I know now!" It's a sad commentary on the lack of preparation for pastors in seminaries. People learn the hard way how to "fight the good fight"; instead of medals they have battle scars and failures to show for their years of hard work. Nobody warned them about what was coming; nobody told them what to expect within the walls of God's house; and they didn't expect to find war *there*. It's no wonder that so many pastors leave the ministry in complete discouragement and even cynicism.

The church is supposed to be the House of God – the house of peace. Why would we go to war in the church? Because we need to know how to stop someone who wants to hurt or destroy the work of Christ's Kingdom (both deliberately or ignorantly). Remember that not everyone in the church is there for the right reasons! And everyone brings some of the world with them into the church.

> Watch out for false prophets. They come to you in sheep's clothing, but inwardly they are ferocious wolves. By their fruit you will recognize them. (Matthew 7:15-16)

Introduction

> I know that after I leave, savage wolves will come in among you and will not spare the flock. Even from your own number men will arise and distort the truth in order to draw away disciples after them. So be on your guard! (Acts 20:29-31)

The famous eighteenth century military commander Frederick the Great once listed several good reasons for waging war:

- To maintain the authority of the kingdom.
- To preserve its security.
- To aid the Kingdom's allies.
- To stop an ambitious troublemaker who works contrary to the interests of the Kingdom's subjects.

These ideas transfer directly to the Church; these are issues that are close to our hearts and affect our Mission. Our enemy fights us from all sides in order to destroy us; he is not only hitting us through the secular world, but he also has his allies within our midst – within the Church walls. And since the enemy won't be easily talked into changing his behavior toward us, we must resort to war to coerce him into leaving us alone. He only understands the sword. So it's time to use that sword against him, with Christ's blessing and training, if we want freedom to live our lives of faith and obedience. It's either that or go back into slavery.

> When you go to war against your enemies and see horses and chariots and an army greater than yours, do not be afraid of them, because the LORD your God, who brought you up out of Egypt, will be with you. (Deuteronomy 20:1)

Leadership

Frederick goes on to say that good men willingly and faithfully defend the citizens of the state, so that the ordinary person can go about his life in peace and prosperity. Jesus says the same thing, only more forcefully as far as the leader's responsibility is concerned.

> The good shepherd lays down his life for the sheep. The hired hand is not the shepherd who owns the sheep. So when he sees the wolf coming, he abandons the sheep and runs away. Then the wolf attacks the flock and scatters it. The man runs away because he is a hired hand and cares nothing for the sheep. (John 10:11-13)

The leader, in other words, *has* to learn war. He is responsible to protect the sheep from the wolves in the world. If you don't want to do this, then you shouldn't be a leader; obviously you don't have the welfare of the sheep at heart.

Being a leader isn't about glory or power; unfortunately a lot of second-rate leaders make a lot of their position but they have little ability to lead the Church. Jesus put it well:

> You know that those who are regarded as rulers of the Gentiles lord it over them, and their high officials exercise authority over them. Not so with you. Instead, whoever wants to become great among you must be your servant, and whoever wants to be first must be slave of all. For even the Son of Man did not come to be served, but to serve, and to give his life as a ransom for many. (Mark 10:42-45)

A leader has two things to accomplish: first, to achieve the Mission that was given him by his Commander; second, to help his followers achieve *their* part in accomplishing that Mission. It's a team effort, and everyone has been called to do their part. Christians have been spiritually equipped to do work in the Church, and the leader has to give them the opportunities they need to fulfill their calling.

What most people don't know is this: the leader's job mainly consists of *solving problems* – because that's what the long road to achieving the Mission is full of! More than anybody else in the Church, the leader is the problem-solver who removes the obstacles along the Church's path in doing God's will. And most of those problems will involve the church members and their struggle against

Introduction

the enemy. So if you are not good at solving problems, or if you don't like doing that, the leadership role is not for you.

War principles

The reason we turn to military science for help is that the army has the same kind of organizational needs, and the same idea of a goal-oriented mission, that the Church has. And the particular problem that the army was specially formed to solve is fighting enemies. Though the Church is busy with much more than fighting with enemies, we certainly have our enemies that we have to deal with as we struggle to achieve our Mission. There are many situations in the life of the Church that require a military-style approach if we hope to solve them. So we can benefit a great deal from learning from the military (though not all ideas will transfer over exactly – we have our own special needs!). The saints in the Bible who successfully fought against their enemies used these proven principles.

The war principles described in this book are specially designed to equip you to meet ministry situations. You may have your own notions on what "war principles" may look like – and perhaps you have very negative impressions of such an idea from your reading or personal experience. If so, you have to separate in your mind the bombs and guns and killing that is part of physical warfare in this world from the *principles* used behind all warfare, spiritual or otherwise. The principles are timeless, and absolutely necessary for any organized effort trying to achieve a goal, or for fighting against resistance or trouble, or for solving problems, or for rescuing those in trouble.[1]

Let's take the problem of Logistics for an example; it's a key factor in waging war successfully. The commander knows that the troops have to be fed and equipped if he wants them to keep fighting. In fact, the problem of supplies is so huge that there has to be an entire department of the army devoted to this task.

---

[1] For instance, you will find that some of the most successful businessmen in the world were once Marines!

Introduction

Jesus, as the consummate Commander, is also concerned about the feeding and provisioning of his troops. Watch as he takes measures to make sure this function of his army is operating well.

> I tell you the truth, unless you eat the flesh of the Son of Man and drink his blood, you have no life in you. Whoever eats my flesh and drinks my blood has eternal life, and I will raise him up at the last day. (John 6:53-54)

> When they had finished eating, Jesus said to Simon Peter, "Simon son of John, do you truly love me more than these?"
> "Yes, Lord," he said, "you know that I love you."
> Jesus said, "Feed my lambs." (John 21:15)

> It was he who gave some to be Apostles, some to be Prophets, some to be evangelists, and some to be pastors and teachers, to prepare God's people for works of service, so that the body of Christ may be built up until we all reach unity in the faith and in the knowledge of the Son of God and become mature, attaining to the whole measure of the fullness of Christ. (Ephesians 4:11-13)

That's Logistics. And if this matter is on Christ's mind, it must be on yours also. Unless you have teachers in place who know how to feed spiritual food to your church members (and are faithful in doing so), those members will not have the strength or wisdom to carry out their own spiritual duties in God's Kingdom. It's that simple. You can ignore Logistics if you want, but the whole church will suffer as a result. But by approaching it methodically, using the principles that the military is so familiar with, you will take care of the spiritual needs of the church.

Train, train, train

It takes rigorous training to see how a battle is shaping up. Many church leaders either don't realize what's going on until it's too late, or they misinterpret the events and target the wrong enemy, or they bring the wrong resources to bear upon the problem. You have to be able to

Introduction

see all the important facets of the spiritual battlefield and take appropriate measures to win the battle. Only the leaders are in the position to do that. Only the prepared and trained leader *can* do that. And even among those in leadership positions, not everyone is going to prove to be an effective leader; the present state of the church is eloquent testimony of that sad fact. If the church is failing, we can lay the blame solidly at the feet of the leaders.ABeremiah speaks of the destruction of Jerusalem in these terms:

> But it happened because of the sins of her prophets and the iniquities of her priests, who shed within her the blood of the righteous. (Lamentations 4:13)

Preparing for war involves much more than the average citizen realizes. The movies about war only show us the troops in the field gallantly defeating the enemy; but the actual scope of the entire war effort is huge – it's like the proverbial hidden 90% of the iceberg. A well-rounded program for preparing for, and achieving, the Mission of the Church would include the following:

Requisite leadership qualities

Church assessment

Leadership and membership training

Logistics – resources and management

Command system

Dealing with problems

Actual warfare against the Enemy – tactics and strategy

Efficient sharing and transfer of leadership

Evaluation and change

We will be discussing each of these areas at length; the fight against the enemy is only a small percentage of the overall effort of organization and training that has to happen in order to insure success in the fight itself. As the leader of the church, you will not only have to be familiar with these areas but skillful at carrying out each one. The church is going to look to you to lead them through these deep waters; that means that you can't afford to be totally ignorant of what you will inevitably run into. You should already be knowledgeable about the issues and be ready to come up with workable solutions – right on the spot. Leadership mistakes are costly in war.

Time for discipline

Is the military model the only way to look at the ministry of the Church? Certainly not! There are many vital aspects to the life of the Church. But the Bible itself spends a great deal of time with the military model, because it is so fruitful an enterprise. There are special needs of the Church that can only be addressed with the military model. And since our generation is so unfamiliar with this outlook, it's time to spend a great deal of time disciplining ourselves with this mindset and gaining the ground back that we have irresponsibly lost to the Enemy.

The Lord Jesus is the Commander-in-Chief of the army of God, and he has assigned officers under him to carry the fight to the enemy. His charge to his officers is plain: to work hard, to study thoroughly, to be courageous, to encourage the troops, and to never give up. Paul's instructions to Timothy (in both books) are a good summary of the Lord's instructions to his officers.

> Fight the good fight of faith. (1 Timothy 6:12)

> Do your best to present yourself to God as one approved, a workman who does not need to be ashamed and who correctly handles the word of truth. (2 Timothy 2:15)

And Joshua, as he was standing on the edge of the Promised Land after his years of training under Moses' leadership, was reminded again of what God expected of him as a leader.

> Be strong and courageous, because you will lead these people to inherit the land I swore to their forefathers to give them. Be strong and very courageous. Be careful to obey all the Law my servant Moses gave you; do not turn from it to the right or to the left, that you may be successful wherever you go. (Joshua 1:6-7)

Introduction

Other books on working in the church tend to focus on other issues, like building up the attendance and community activities and such. This book, however, is for you, the leader. Design the church right from the ground up, follow the principles rigorously, lead the church in the right direction doing the right things, and you have good reason to expect success in your ministry.

Introduction

THE BIBLE AND WAR

Israel's God is a God of war, and he expects his people to take up arms to defeat our enemies and establish his Kingdom. When you read the Bible in this light, it's easy to see our duty and get motivated to do our part in the struggle against the forces of darkness.

THE BIBLE AND WAR

Among other things, the Bible is a war manual. In its pages we read about the history of the wars of the Israelite nation, generals and troops, strategy and tactics, victories and defeats, armies and enemies clashing all through the Middle East. The New Testament carries the subject to a deeper level, on a cosmic scope, with eternal consequences. Most Christians use the Bible on the lowest possible level – just a book of promises and "feel-good" maxims when they need some encouragement; but for those who need specific instruction about war, the Bible is a tremendous resource.

Forced into war

Though there are many students of war who are fascinated by the art and science of the subject, it's not fascination that drives Christians to study it. The Prophet said that one day we Christians will beat our swords back into ploughshares; that's our ultimate goal. We are people of peace.

But we can't afford that luxury right now. Our enemies are attacking us from all sides, and the world at large is being destroyed at an alarming rate. And strangely, while the war rages around us, so many Christians are often in denial that there's any war going on at all!

The Bible, however, gives us a wake-up call about the necessity of going to a war-footing:

> Then Moses said to them, "If you will do this — if you will arm yourselves before the LORD for battle, and if all of you will go armed over the Jordan before the LORD until he has driven his enemies out before him — then when the land is subdued before the LORD, you may return and be free from your obligation to the LORD and to Israel. And this

land will be your possession before the LORD." (Numbers 32:20-22)

> Finally, be strong in the Lord and in his mighty power. Put on the full armor of God so that you can take your stand against the devil's schemes. (Ephesians 6:10-11)

In other words, it's not a suggestion but a command. Every Christian is called to war; every believer is threatened, and everyone is needed for the effort. If anybody rejects the King's call to war, that person will be cut off and left to the "tender mercies" of the enemy.

> A proclamation was then issued throughout Judah and Jerusalem for all the exiles to assemble in Jerusalem. Anyone who failed to appear within three days would forfeit all his property, in accordance with the decision of the officials and elders, and would himself be expelled from the assembly of the exiles. (Ezra 10:7-8)

Reasons for war

War threatens our peace, our social structure, our prosperity and safety. It brings death and destruction and misery in its wake. And though we might not want to be drawn into a fight, someone else will force it upon us. The only options will be either to go down in defeat, or to fight back.

For Christians, we have spiritual treasures that we can't do without, such as our union with God, the Truth, fellowship with the saints. And we also have enemies who are desperately trying to wreck those treasures or separate us from them. This is unacceptable, because our spiritual life depends on them. Take them away and we can't survive spiritually.

As long as we are in this world, we are in danger of losing touch with our spiritual treasures. Jesus promised to be our strength and refuge, but the enemy has ways of convincing us to move away from the Lord – it's our own waywardness that is the problem here.

Recognizing that, Jesus prayed for his people that they might be protected from the evil one and stay on course.

> My prayer is not that you take them out of the world but that you protect them from the evil one. They are not of the world, even as I am not of it. Sanctify them by the truth; your word is truth. (John 17:15-17)

Far from encouraging us to be complacent about our spiritual standing, Jesus warned us that we will always be in the middle of a raging war over our souls. He himself is ready to do battle to protect us.

> Do not suppose that I have come to bring peace to the earth. I did not come to bring peace, but a sword. (Matthew 10:34)

God has nothing but disgust for leaders who tell their followers that there's no such war going on.

> From the least to the greatest, all are greedy for gain; prophets and priests alike, all practice deceit. They dress the wound of my people as though it were not serious. 'Peace, peace,' they say, when there is no peace. (Jeremiah 6:13-14)

So in keeping with the message of the Prophets, we have to emphasize that we are in the middle of a desperate spiritual struggle, and we are at great risk before the ruthless wrath of the enemy who wants to undermine the grace that we have received from our God. There are at least five areas that we have to turn our attention to.

1. Our lifeline to God

Vital Christianity is being in touch with God himself: Jesus said that to know God, personally, is our very life. If we lose contact with God, we wither inside spiritually. Our zeal grows cold, we live in the darkness, we are more prone to temptation and sin, and we become amazingly vulnerable to the Enemy. God gives us *everything* we need for life and godliness. We can't afford to lose touch with him, because all sorts of damaging effects will show up.

> I sink in the miry depths, where there is no foothold. I have come into the deep waters; the floods engulf me. I am worn out calling for help; my throat is parched. My eyes fail, looking for my God. (Psalm 60:30-31)

To show how vital it is to stay in touch with God, he shows his displeasure with someone by backing away from them and leaving them on their own. This is our greatest fear – not to be heard or helped by God.

> Although they fast, I will not listen to their cry; though they offer burnt offerings and grain offerings, I will not accept them. (Jeremiah 14:12)

> You do not have, because you do not ask God. When you ask, you do not receive, because you ask with wrong motives, that you may spend what you get on your pleasures. (James 4:2-3)

2. Our resources at risk

If you lose touch with God, the spiritual resources that you need to survive spiritually in this world will disappear or seriously diminish. For example, the Temple was the source of all that the Israelites needed from their God: their protection, their wisdom, their joy, their focus and purpose in life, their strength, the will of God. When their enemies destroyed the Temple, therefore, they knew they were an easy kill for the enemy – their God was gone, along with every good thing that God provides for his people.

> Your foes roared in the place where you met with us; they set up their standards as signs. They behaved like men wielding axes to cut through a

thicket of trees. They smashed all the carved paneling with their axes and hatchets. They burned your sanctuary to the ground; they defiled the dwelling place of your Name. They said in their hearts, "We will crush them completely!" They burned every place where God was worshiped in the land. We are given no miraculous signs; no prophets are left, and none of us knows how long this will be. (Psalm 74:4-9)

Christians value their relationship with God, and the spiritual treasures that were promised them. Our security and peace of heart, understanding and wisdom, individual and church blessings, salvation from sin – we have so much at our disposal. Many Christians don't realize, however, that the things they value can easily disappear – not that God has disappeared, but access to him and all that treasure can be cut off by the enemy. The enemy is good at getting between us and God. It can be remedied, but it requires doing battle against a determined enemy who would rather see us die than be restored to fellowship with God.

> Even if I summoned him and he responded, I do not believe he would give me a hearing. (Job 9:16)

> My people are destroyed from lack of knowledge. (Hosea 4:6)

3. Destructive temptations

The world is full of temptations that are killing the pagans; but the Christian is supposed to be able to resist those temptations. When he has lost his protection, however, the simplest sins can ruin his life, his reputation, his family, and his work. He finds out too late that God was protecting him from every sin, no matter how small, because the sins of the world are deadly even in the smallest doses.

> So I find this law at work: When I want to do good, evil is right there with me. For in my inner being I delight in God's Law; but I see another law at work in the members of my body, waging war against the law of my mind and making me a prisoner of the law of sin at work within my members. What a wretched man I am! Who will rescue me from this body of death? (Romans 7:21-24)

David, when he fell to the temptation of lust, ended up in the middle of a moral and political disaster. He knew the trouble he had caused, and he was soon to learn the trouble that was yet to come upon his family and the nation because of his lapse into immorality.

> Have mercy on me, O God, according to your unfailing love; according to your great compassion blot out my transgressions. Wash away all my iniquity and cleanse me from my sin. For I know my transgressions, and my sin is always before me. Against you, you only, have I sinned and done what is evil in your sight, so that you are proved right when you speak and justified when you judge. (Psalm 51:1-4)

4. Neighbors dead and dying

Just across the fence from you are people who are being destroyed by these deadly enemies that you may or may not be taking seriously. Even if life is good for you, your neighbor is suffering with his problems. It's hard to believe what many people go through in this life; in fact, many people doubt that God is really in control of things in light of what so many people have to endure. But the physical problems are only the symptoms; the real enemies are rotting away the hearts of most people in the world, with the result that billions are going to be destroyed on Judgment Day. Without the necessary spiritual foundations that Christ gives sinners, they will inevitably fall.

Yes, we Christians are safe in Christ; but doesn't it make you think when you see so many others around you who are still living in darkness and with no hope? What has God done for you! And what yet needs to be done in the world?

> You will not fear the terror of night, nor the arrow that flies by day, nor the pestilence that stalks in the darkness, nor the plague that destroys at midday. A thousand may fall at your side, ten thousand at your right hand, but it will not come near you. You will only observe with your eyes and see the punishment of the wicked. (Psalm 91:5-8)

> So I tell you this, and insist on it in the Lord, that you must no longer live as the Gentiles do, in the futility of their thinking. They are darkened in their understanding and separated from the life of God because of the ignorance that is in them due to the hardening of their hearts. Having lost all sensitivity, they have given themselves over to sensuality so as to indulge in every kind of impurity, with a continual lust for more. (Ephesians 4:17-19)

5. Assaults of the enemy

The Church everywhere in the world is being persecuted, though it may not appear that way from our comfortable seats here in America. Outward persecution, as the Apostles experienced it, is the norm in many countries; other ideologies hate the principles of Christianity and will institute destructive measures to destroy it or immobilize it. What Americans don't seem to realize yet, however, is that our three main enemies are eating away at our Christian testimony to the point that it has lost its power in *our* culture. The spiritual descendants of the Moabites have been busy undermining the Church in our country, leading believers into immorality and materialism. Christians have become just as dirty with the world's filth as the pagans are, and they don't seem to see anything wrong with that.

> While Israel was staying in Shittim, the men began to indulge in sexual immorality with Moabite women, who invited them to the sacrifices to their gods. The people ate and bowed down before these gods. So Israel joined in worshiping the Baal of Peor. And the LORD's anger burned against them. (Numbers 25:1-3)

When Christians realize, as they do from time to time, that they have become too lax in their standards and they decide to discipline themselves for God's service, the friction between them and the world gets worse; it's inevitable. The more holy we become, the more the world will hate us. So the very thing we want to see – revival in today's Church – is going to be the call to war.

> They called the Apostles in and had them flogged. Then they ordered them not to speak in the name of Jesus, and let them go. (Acts 5:40)

The nature of our enemies – get this right!

The first task in war is to properly identify the enemy. There are two steps here: we have to identify the *right* enemy, and we have to admit that they *are* the enemy.

This is a critical step in the Church for several reasons. First, we tend to identify the wrong enemies and end up fighting against each other. There's a difference between our spiritual enemies and the poor dupes who are being used by them! Even Peter was used by the Enemy, though Jesus dealt with him sternly as a result. (Mark 8:33)

Our real enemies are deadly, they never give up, and our goal must be nothing less than their total destruction.

- ### The heart

    Otherwise known as the "flesh", or that part of us that responds to – no, positively *lusts* for – the temptations of pleasure and power. Our own hearts have led us blithely into ruinous temptations and have met with hardly any resistance along the way. Even those who know better are guilty of willingly feeding their lusts.

    > The heart is deceitful above all things and beyond cure. Who can understand it? (Jeremiah 17:9)

    The heart is the inner man, the unsanctified flesh that cries out for pleasure and comfort, that rebels against command and restraint. Usually people keep it under control when they are in public – we can't usually tell the true nature of a person from looking at the outside. But in time, what they really are will come out in their words, desires, thoughts and actions, as they take measures to feed their lusts and desires.

    > But the things that come out of the mouth come from the heart, and these make a man 'unclean.' For out of the heart come evil thoughts, murder, adultery, sexual immorality, theft, false testimony, slander. These are what make a man 'unclean'. (Matthew 15:18-20)

    The greatest of the world as well as the least have fallen to the lusts of the flesh. Adam and Eve led the way; Moses fell to the sin of self-glory; Jacob's sons as well as David,

Solomon, and so many others fell to the lusts of the flesh. Pride, ambition, hard-heartedness, anger and wrath, selfishness, rebellion – these kinds of sins are built into our nature, and we nurture them because we get what we want from them. The problem is that they are so destructive of our lives; we may get short-term pleasure and profit from them, but in the long run they destroy us and those around us. It's deadly to keep entertaining these tendencies.

- **The World**

> Do not love the world or anything in the world. If anyone loves the world, the love of the Father is not in him. For everything in the world — the cravings of sinful man, the lust of his eyes and the boasting of what he has and does — comes not from the Father but from the world. The world and its desires pass away, but the man who does the will of God lives forever. (1 John 2:15-17)

God made the world to be "very good" (Genesis 1:31), but when Adam and Eve rebelled against God they began remaking the world into *their* own image. In other words, what kind of world will best satisfy their lusts and desires? Every generation tries to form a new world that will please them: full of riches and comfort, temptations and opportunities to lust, destruction and repression of the weak and victory and power to the strong. Business, government, politics, sports and entertainment, education – we have built up a complex and creative world around us that will give us lots of opportunities to feed the flesh.

But though we keep trying, we can't re-make this world into what we want without causing a great deal of pain and suffering. When we try to bend it to suit us, we end up breaking something. For example, all of our technological achievements have only caused a widespread social disaster: the Internet, as potential as it might appear, is the biggest purveyor of porn and sexual immorality on the planet. Every "good" thing that we invent seems to have a downside. Factories that produce cars and computers pollute the environment; video games cause slavery conditions in third-world countries as companies scramble to produce the rare-earth ingredients for the electronics; medicines end up forcing the bacteria and viruses to become drug resistant. So in the end, when you balance everything together, we have achieved nothing but trouble.

> I denied myself nothing my eyes desired; I refused my heart no pleasure. My heart took delight in all my work, and this was the reward for all my labor. Yet when I surveyed all that my hands had done and what I had toiled to achieve, everything was meaningless, a chasing after the wind; nothing was gained under the sun. (Ecclesiastes 2:10-11)

- **Satan**

    > As for you, you were dead in your transgressions and sins, in which you used to live when you followed the ways of this world and of the ruler of the kingdom of the air, the spirit who is now at work in those who are disobedient. (Ephesians 2:1-2)

    > Be self-controlled and alert. Your enemy the devil prowls around like a roaring lion looking for someone to devour. Resist him, standing firm in the faith, because you know that your brothers throughout the world are undergoing the same kind of sufferings. (1 Peter 5:8-9)

    An ancient enemy (he was there in the beginning with Adam and Eve), Satan has a profound hatred of God and anything made in God's image. He specializes in deceit and death: where there are lies, there is Satan; where there is wanton destruction, especially self-destruction, there is the influence of the devil. He covers himself to disguise his presence, often "masquerading as an angel of light" to better deceive us. And he clothes himself with pride: he will not submit to God.

He was there in the Garden of Eden to permanently cripple the human race from the very beginning. Satan shows his animosity toward us and toward God in the book of Job; he is always looking for opportunities to destroy us. He tried to destroy Jesus after his baptism; he hounded Jesus throughout his ministry; though hiding in the darkness, he was continually uncovered by Jesus as the Lord delivered many people from demonic possession. The Apostles were fully aware of his activities and counseled the churches to take up arms to resist him. And in the book of Revelation we read the story of the great battle raging between the forces of Heaven and Satan, when finally our great enemy will be destroyed for eternity in the lake of fire.

> And the devil, who deceived them, was thrown into the lake of burning sulfur, where the beast and the false prophet had been thrown. They will be tormented day and night for ever and ever. (Revelation 20:10)

In order to defeat these enemies, much less keep from being destroyed by them, it will require not only determination but a great deal of study on the part of the leaders. "Know your enemy" is still the wisest counsel for potential church leaders; only by knowing him fully can you intelligently fight against him.

- **More troubles**

Besides these three enemies, we have other troublemakers of various types that give us problems on an individual level as well as on the Church level.

> Jesus turned and said to Peter, "Get behind me, Satan! You are a stumbling block to me; you do not

have in mind the things of God, but the things of men." (Matthew 16:23)

This passage refers to ignorant Christians who mean well but end up ruining things if we follow their advice. They don't know the true state of things: they may be "baby" Christians, or they may not have grown enough spiritually to understand God's will on a matter. They have to be put in their places (Paul counsels us to do it gently but firmly!); we can't cater to their wishes just to make them feel a part of things. The Mission comes before people's feelings.

> So I tell you this, and insist on it in the Lord, that you must no longer live as the Gentiles do, in the futility of their thinking. They are darkened in their understanding and separated from the life of God because of the ignorance that is in them due to the hardening of their hearts. Having lost all sensitivity, they have given themselves over to sensuality so as to indulge in every kind of impurity, with a continual lust for more. (Ephesians 4:17-19)

> They have become filled with every kind of wickedness, evil, greed and depravity. They are full of envy, murder, strife, deceit and malice. They are gossips, slanderers, God-haters, insolent, arrogant and boastful; they invent ways of doing evil; they disobey their parents; they are senseless, faithless, heartless, ruthless. (Romans 1:29-31)

These passages refer to ordinary "pagans" who don't believe in God and they live like it. Morals don't exist for them; they live simply to satisfy their passions. They will either not be interested in your faith, or they will obstruct you in some way because you are interfering with them. They don't particularly have an agenda to destroy Christianity, but they won't hesitate to lend their weight to stopping the Church if they feel that the Church is getting in the way of their immorality and lust.

> For certain men whose condemnation was written about long ago have secretly slipped in among you. They are godless men, who change the grace of our God into a license for immorality and deny Jesus Christ our only Sovereign and Lord. (Jude 4)

> You suffered from your own countrymen the same things those churches suffered from the Jews, who killed the Lord Jesus and the prophets and also drove us out. They displease God and are hostile to all men in their effort to keep us from speaking to the Gentiles so that they may be saved. In this way they always heap up their sins to the limit. The wrath of God has come upon them at last. (1 Thessalonians 2:14-16)

> These last passages talk about those who are determined to destroy Christianity. These people know what Christians are all about, and they are out to deliberately wreck the work of the Church. They will even disguise themselves as friends of the Church in order to "worm their way in" for a better kill. These are the wolves that both Jesus and Paul warned us about – preying on the sheep of Christ's flock.

How did God respond to his enemies in the Bible? He punished Adam and Eve, and all of their progeny, with death for rebellion against his Word (Genesis 4); he destroyed immoral pagans all around the world with the Flood during Noah's day (Genesis 6-8); he threw Satan out of Heaven along with all the other angels siding with the dark spirit of rebellion (Revelation 12:9); he dethroned Saul for disobedience (1 Samuel 15); he divided the nation of Israel into two warring factions because of Solomon's idolatries (1 Kings 11); he crushed Egypt for resisting Moses and the Israelites (Exodus 7-12); he sent his own people into a 70-year exile for worshiping false gods (2 Chronicles 36). Actually the list could go on and on. God has shown himself to be a God of war, ruthlessly defeating his enemies who want to deny his authority and power and build their own world apart from him.

Old Testament war – the model

In the Old Testament we get a clear description of what it's like to be in God's army. First of all, we find out that there is a real war going on and there are definite sides; the question is which side we want to be on. The descendants of Abraham are God's people, and everyone else is the enemy. The war begins with the story of Israel coming together as a nation under Moses at Mt. Sinai, continues with the entering of the Promised Land and the destruction of the Canaanites living there, the struggles with the remaining pagan nations leading them in idolatry, David's summary defeat of the enemies of Israel, the Exile and the refining of the Remnant, the Return of the Exiles to start again in Jerusalem, and the spiritual Remnant that Jesus raises up from the dead. At the very end, only the spiritual descendants of Abraham will win the war and finally enter into their rest in eternity.

In the Old Testament we read about armies and commanders. Moses and Joshua led the Israelites in many battles against their enemies, using strategies and tactics designed by God to utterly annihilate their enemies. The Judges led the Israelites in battle against the nations who were oppressing them. David was a master at warfare, and several of his descendants were also expert commanders who defended Jerusalem successfully. And then there were those times when God allowed Israel's enemies to win: both Assyria and Babylon overwhelmed God's people and hauled them away in shame into exile. These are set-pieces of warfare that would be good material for study.

And war in the Old Testament was ruthless. If there is a major difference between war in those days and war now, we could say that our modern war principles have struggled to make war more "humane" and limited in its scope. I suppose the idea is that we don't want to alienate these so-called enemies permanently; if we win, we want them to change sides and try to get along with us. After all, aren't they like us – just ordinary people forced by politicians into a war they don't really want to fight? But in the Old Testament, the point was to *annihilate the enemy*. Whole cities were totally destroyed: not only all the men, women and children, but the animals as well. God often punished his commanders for being "humane" and not following through on these orders. To God, the issue was deeper than political or social issues: the pagans hated him, loved immorality and rebellion, and deserved to die. Even their infants, in God's eyes, were pagans in the making.

Of course there were people in those days who also failed to take war seriously, just as we often do. They let their guard down, thinking the situation was safe enough and they had an opportunity to relax. They learned painfully that the enemy never relaxes; he is looking for those moments when we carelessly lay our weapons down. David, for example, fell into adultery and murder on a comfortable evening. In Ezekiel the watchmen are warned to *never* relax their vigilance; if they fail to sound the alarm when the enemy shows up, the blood of the innocent will be on their heads.

> When I bring the sword against a land, and the people of the land choose one of their men and make him their watchman, and he sees the sword coming against the land and blows the trumpet to warn the people, then if anyone hears the trumpet but does not take warning and the sword comes and takes his life, his blood will be on his own head. Since he heard the sound of the trumpet but did not take warning, his blood will be on his own head. If he had taken warning, he would have saved himself. But if the watchman sees the sword coming and does not blow the trumpet to warn the people and the sword comes and takes the life of one of them, that man will be taken away because of his sin, but I will hold the watchman accountable for his blood. (Ezekiel 33:1-6)

New Testament war

While everyone would agree that the Old Testament is full of war, most people like to think that the scene changes with the arrival of the "gentle Shepherd" and now we enter a period of peace. That is *not* true! War breaks out as soon as Jesus is born. Herod, you will remember, sent soldiers to kill all the infants in Bethlehem to make sure he destroyed the predicted Messiah (a mission he failed in, thankfully!). The entire ministry of Christ was a series of battles against the forces of darkness (Satan and evil spirits) and the Pharisees who were fighting him every step of the way. His crucifixion seemed to be a victory for his enemies, but his resurrection pulled victory from the jaws of defeat and instead sent his enemies permanently reeling back. Now in the Church age he passes the battle on to us and calls us to keep fighting to extend his Kingdom.

His war tactics aren't what you would expect to win a fight, but they are amazingly effective in this kind of war. Forgiving your brother seventy-seven times absolutely shuts down the possibility of condemnation and back-stabbing in the Church. Winning the lost through evangelism targets the real enemy – Satan – and treats our neighbors (irritating though they may be!) as they really are, dupes of the enemy who need to be brought back from the dead and given real life. These and other tactics are the only effective way to achieve the Mission.

Now that Jesus is sitting on his throne in Heaven, he continues to direct his Church in battles against the enemy. Satan and his cohorts are still battling the Church, in forms of temptations, persecutions, ignorance, a broken world, and nasty neighbors. The Apostles showed us how to build up our strongholds to fight this fight of faith; we learn about the refuge we have in Christ, the weapons that we have to fight with, encouragements to persevere, methods of rescuing victims from the enemy's ranks, the need for discipline, guarding ourselves from wolves within our own ranks, the victory crown for those who are faithful to the end, and the penalty for traitors and cowards. The final battle – Armageddon – will settle the issue once and for all; only then will we be able to lay our swords down and fight no more.

Counsel about war

There are many passages that counsel us to take war seriously. Here are just a few that you would do well to think on.

> Be self-controlled and alert. (1 Peter 5:8)

> I am sending you out like sheep among wolves. Therefore be as shrewd as snakes and as innocent as doves.

Be on your guard against men; they will hand you over to the local councils and flog you in their synagogues. On my account you will be brought before governors and kings as witnesses to them and to the Gentiles. (Matthew 10:17-18)

Watch out for false prophets. They come to you in sheep's clothing, but inwardly they are ferocious wolves. By their fruit you will recognize them. (Matthew 7:15)

Finally, be strong in the Lord and in his mighty power. Put on the full armor of God so that you can take your stand against the devil's schemes. For our struggle is not against flesh and blood, but against the rulers, against the authorities, against the powers of this dark world and against the spiritual forces of evil in the Heavenly realms. Therefore put on the full armor of God, so that when the day of evil comes, you may be able to stand your ground, and after you have done everything, to stand. (Ephesians 6:10-13)

Be very careful, then, how you live — not as unwise but as wise, making the most of every opportunity, because the days are evil. Therefore do not be foolish, but understand what the Lord's will is. (Ephesians 5:15-17)

But you are not to be called 'Rabbi,' for you have only one Master and you are all brothers. And do not call anyone on earth 'father,' for you have one Father, and he is in Heaven. Nor are you to be called 'teacher,' for you have one Teacher, the Christ. (Matthew 23:8-10)[2]

Do not store up for yourselves treasures on earth, where moth and rust destroy, and where thieves break in and steal. But store up for yourselves treasures in Heaven, where moth

---

[2] This passage has to do with the Commander of the army of God; Jesus reserves complete authority and power over his Church, and we are here simply to follow his will. We will win our battles only if we obey him completely and passionately. And we follow our church leaders only when they follow Christ's orders exactly.

and rust do not destroy, and where thieves do not break in and steal. (Matthew 6:19-20)

For this very reason, make every effort to add to your faith goodness; and to goodness, knowledge; and to knowledge, self-control; and to self-control, perseverance; and to perseverance, godliness; and to godliness, brotherly kindness; and to brotherly kindness, love. For if you possess these qualities in increasing measure, they will keep you from being ineffective and unproductive in your knowledge of our Lord Jesus Christ. But if anyone does not have them, he is nearsighted and blind, and has forgotten that he has been cleansed from his past sins. (2 Peter 1:5-9)

Be diligent in these matters; give yourself wholly to them, so that everyone may see your progress. Watch your life and doctrine closely. Persevere in them, because if you do, you will save both yourself and your hearers. (1 Timothy 4:15-16)

These passages and more cover all the aspects of war: logistics, discipline, strategy and tactics, weaponry, offense and defense, knowing the enemy, character and faithfulness. As you can see, God doesn't give us the option to go back home and refuse the fight. He is presently out on the battlefield and he has called all of his people out to the field to fight with him. Our only duty is to obey the Commander and arm ourselves for battle.

War strategies and tactics

When I first started studying war, all I could understand was the fighting part: people aimed guns at each other and started firing, and people died and some won the battles. But when I started studying the principles of warfare, I went back to those same history books and recognized military strategy and tactics – *what* they were doing and *why* they were doing it made so much more sense to me.

The same is true with the Bible. To those who are completely ignorant of military principles, the Bible can be a confusing collection of stories that don't make much sense. But with some training, the real lessons come out clearly. We watch the Lord moving his people to Canaan, then down to Egypt (the Commander is moving his troops into position for battle, getting them ready for the final move back to Canaan), out into the wilderness, and then into the Promised Land. We watch the Lord setting up lines of communication for his people so that they can survive in the wilderness. He directs assaults against the enemy using tactics designed to catch them off their guard and trap them. He uses deception against his enemies, keeping them in the dark about his true motives; see for example the stories of Rahab and Joshua's fighting tactics.

It's been said that war brings out both the best and the worst in men. Read through Proverbs some time and you will see character studies of both the best and the worst. God needs us to change if we are to be of any use to him. Fools and the wicked and the immoral and cowards and the lazy are doomed to be destroyed, since they are obviously on the wrong side. But the wise, the righteous, the courageous, the diligent and the faithful will be of great service in God's army and will reap great rewards for their service.

Jesus also, being the Commander of the Church, uses Biblical methods in his campaign against the forces of darkness. His goal is to rescue his people from sin and death and bring them into the Eternal Kingdom. So he trains an invasion force (it took three years to train his disciples – typical for a military officer's training) to assault the enemy's lines and take prisoners. He supplies and trains and disciplines his troops. He builds walls of defense against the enemies who would attack his Church. He even has military police keeping watch on the camp itself to alert the Church to internal enemies.

> Now you are the body of Christ, and each one of you is a part of it. And in the church God has appointed first of all Apostles, second Prophets, third teachers, then workers of miracles, also those having gifts of healing, those able to help others, those with gifts of administration, and those speaking in different kinds of tongues. (1 Corinthians 12:27-28)

To the trained eye, there is so much in the Bible that corresponds exactly to the principles of warfare that it would be criminal for the church leaders to ignore all of this. We therefore should spend time studying this military textbook to get the most out of its lessons.

The Commander

God does so many things, he plays so many roles in his universe, that we tend to overlook some of his most important roles and focus only on those things that most interest us. It's comforting and encouraging to see him as our loving Father; but don't forget that he is also the Lord of Hosts.

> The LORD is a warrior; the LORD is his name. Pharaoh's chariots and his army he has hurled into the sea. The best of Pharaoh's officers are drowned in the Red Sea. (Exodus 15:3-4)

> I saw Heaven standing open and there before me was a white horse, whose rider is called Faithful and True. With justice he judges and makes war. His eyes are like blazing fire, and on his head are many crowns. He has a name written on him that no one knows but he himself. He is dressed in a robe dipped in blood, and his name is the Word of God. The armies of Heaven were following him, riding on white horses and dressed in fine linen, white and clean. Out of his mouth comes a sharp sword with which to strike down the nations. "He will rule them with an iron scepter." He treads the winepress of the fury of the wrath of God Almighty. On his robe and on his thigh he has this name written: KING OF KINGS AND LORD OF LORDS. (Revelation 19:11-16)

There are times when we need his gentle hand taking care of us. But there are other times when we have to get dressed for battle and show up on the field ready to do our duty. He is there already, expecting us, and now is not the time for comforting words. It's the time for discipline and duty and doing our part to win the Kingdom for Christ.

Our God is a Commander. He has all authority – for the very good reason that he intends to command all the troops, arrange the battle plans, train the troops, organize the logistics and engineering needed, lead the charge against the enemy and win the day. And like an army commander, the only thing he wants from us is a "yes sir!"

> All authority in Heaven and on earth has been given to me. (Matthew 28:18)

He is called the "Wonderful Counselor" because he knows what you need, when you need it, and how you are to use it. He knows what everyone needs; he is the consummate project manager, skillfully organizing every aspect of his army down to the last detail, and timing every single event perfectly to achieve the Mission. He has a heart for his troops; he provides for them, he heals their wounds, he treats them as brothers. His goal is to save them from this world; the purpose of this war, after all, is to rescue them from death and give them a life of bliss with God. This whole effort of his is only for them.

Jesus is totally focused on the Mission. Like a commander who believes in the cause, he can't be diverted from the Mission. He set his face toward Jerusalem like flint; he had no interest in politics or business or even family matters. But he had all the time in the world for sinners needing his help, for the lowly who had no one else to turn to. He prepared his entire life for this Mission; and when at the end he laid down his life, he was satisfied that he had perfectly and completely fulfilled his calling.

And because he was so disciplined and passionate about the Mission, he had no time for those who weren't. If people weren't interested in what he had to offer them, he shook the dust off his feet and went to the next town. If the leaders resisted him, he embarrassed them in public and counseled his followers to ignore such leaders. When he trained his disciples, he required the same single-minded devotion to the Mission that he had: it's time to leave family behind if necessary, the riches of the world, the world's various callings, and work for a better world.

> As Jesus went on from there, he saw a man named Matthew sitting at the tax collector's booth. "Follow me," he told him, and Matthew got up and followed him. (Matthew 9:9)

> Anyone who loves his father or mother more than me is not worthy of me; anyone who loves his son or daughter more than me is not worthy of me; and anyone who does not take his cross and follow me is not worthy of me. (Matthew 10:37-38)

Better to die fighting this battle than to live relaxing in the emptiness of this world.

> If anyone would come after me, he must deny himself and take up his cross and follow me. For whoever wants to save his life will lose it, but whoever loses his life for me will find it. What good will it be for a man if he gains the whole world, yet forfeits his soul? Or what can a man give in exchange for his soul? (Matthew 16:24-26)

Leaders

There are a few people who are born with the skills of leadership, but even they have to undergo extensive training to fine-tune their skills and give them the experience they need in leadership roles. Most of us, however, have to start at the beginning and learn the basics of being a successful leader.

The leaders of the Bible were all trained by God for their respective roles. There's an important reason for this: God is building a spiritual Kingdom, and there are requirements that are qualitatively different from those necessary for a physical Kingdom. The most important requirement, of course, is that in all things God must get glory. That's not something we naturally know how to do! Only God can show us, and enable us, to give him the credit he deserves and let him do his part without interference from us.

Moses, for example, learned that there are certain things only God can do – there were times when he learned to step back and let God lead.

> Moses answered the people, "Do not be afraid. Stand firm and you will see the deliverance the LORD will bring you today. The Egyptians you see today you will never see again. The LORD will fight for you; you need only to be still." (Exodus 14:13-14)

When he forgot this (the time when he disobeyed God on how to give water to the Israelites), he paid a heavy penalty.

> Because you did not trust in me enough to honor me as holy in the sight of the Israelites, you will not bring this community into the land I give them. (Numbers 20:12)

Leaders in God's Church have to learn the Ways of the Lord, the Works of the Lord, the Names of the Lord – in order to work with God and not against him. These are resources and reserves that God has provided for his people. Leaders have to not only learn the lessons of the Bible but practice them over and over until they are skilled in the knowledge and wisdom of God. Moses knew God's Ways and succeeded (though the rest of the Israelites didn't learn them until the second generation). Saul had no idea of what God's Ways were, and therefore failed as a leader. Joseph knew them and fulfilled a key role in the survival of Jacob's little but important family.

There are leaders who can manage grand projects and there are others who can only handle smaller assignments. Napoleon knew that not all of his subordinate officers were capable of handling armies, so he assigned them to the jobs that they *were* capable of. Moses, though he was enabled to lead all of Israel through the desert, needed a lot of help from minor officials who could take the burden of daily jurisdiction off his shoulders.

> He chose capable men from all Israel and made them leaders of the people, officials over thousands, hundreds, fifties and tens. They served as judges for the people at all

times. The difficult cases they brought to Moses, but the simple ones they decided themselves. (Exodus 18:25-26)

David ruled over Israel and fixed the national problems in a way that his predecessor Saul could not; but he couldn't be everywhere at once. So he appointed minor officials who executed his will all over the country in the cities and towns. And they were instructed to carry out the Mission, in their own spheres, as David understood it.

Jesus trained his disciples, but in ways that to this day perplexes the experts. He counseled them to serve others, not lord it over them; he showed them how to do without the things in this world that most people take for granted; he led them *into* persecution and oppression from the enemy; he advised them to give their possessions to others so as to win rewards in Heaven. His economics were opposite the principles of this world, his tactics were seemingly designed to lose battles, and his values were little appreciated. But he consistently won his battles using such methods, and his disciples found by experience that they would win also if they remained faithful to his teaching. Thus the Church was successfully started on a foundation of a new breed of leaders that this world had never seen before. Its present leaders – elders and deacons and those with spiritual gifts – carry on the fight that the original Apostles began and paved the way for.

Troops

Leaders and commanders may do the thinking, but the real fight is between the troops out on the battlefield. Without the leader the troops are confused and lost; but without troops there can be no war.

Actually the leaders can suffer under a serious misconception about their own role in a war: they are there only to *help the troops achieve the objective*. The troops don't exist for the leaders; rather the leaders exist for the troops.

So there is a heavy emphasis in the Bible about the spiritual state, preparedness, and faithfulness of the average Christian. Without this the Church cannot stand. Most of the fighting will be done on the individual level, as we all struggle against the flesh, the world and the devil with the resources God has given us.

This is why we have the Bible counseling us about preparing for battle.

> Therefore, prepare your minds for action; be self-controlled; set your hope fully on the grace to be given you when Jesus Christ is revealed. As obedient children, do not conform to the evil desires you had when you lived in ignorance. But just as he who called you is holy, so be holy in all you do; for it is written: "Be holy, because I am holy." (1 Peter 1:13-16)

> For this very reason, make every effort to add to your faith goodness; and to goodness, knowledge; and to knowledge, self-control; and to self-control, perseverance; and to perseverance, godliness; and to godliness, brotherly kindness; and to brotherly kindness, love. For if you possess these qualities in increasing measure, they will keep you from being ineffective and unproductive in your knowledge of our Lord Jesus Christ. (2 Peter 1:5-8)

A soldier has to equip himself with defensive and offensive weapons, and be trained in the use of them.

> Finally, be strong in the Lord and in his mighty power. Put on the full armor of God so that you can take your stand against the devil's schemes. For our struggle is not against flesh and blood, but against the rulers, against the authorities, against the powers of this dark world and against the spiritual forces of evil in the heavenly realms. Therefore put on the full armor of God, so that when the day of evil comes, you may be able to stand your ground, and after you have done everything, to stand. (Ephesians 6:10-13)

And, though he will not learn the art of war to the extent that the leaders do, he too must know something of the enemy's ways and tactics, so that he can move quickly in the middle of battle, defend himself, and take advantages of opportunities.

> Be very careful, then, how you live — not as unwise but as wise, making the most of every opportunity, because the days are evil. Therefore do not be foolish, but understand what the Lord's will is. (Ephesians 5:15-17)

> Be self-controlled and alert. Your enemy the devil prowls around like a roaring lion looking for someone to devour. (1 Peter 5:8)

The Commander will not be pleased with an excuse like "But I didn't know!"

> His master replied, "You wicked, lazy servant! So you knew that I harvest where I have not sown and gather where I have not scattered seed?" ... "Throw that worthless servant outside, into the darkness, where there will be weeping and gnashing of teeth." (Matthew 25:26,30)

We are to keep diligent watch over our most sensitive areas, the special targets that our enemies love to hit. We have special armor and defensive skills to protect those areas. If you fail here, you will die in battle.

> Above all else, guard your heart, for it is the wellspring of life. (Proverbs 4:23)

And the Bible is very plain about our relationship to our leaders: obedience to the will of God is paramount. The army of God can't exist on rebellion and self-will; God will not permit insurrection in his ranks. There can be only one will in his army.

> You are my friends if you do what I command. (John 15:14)

> Obey your leaders and submit to their authority. They keep watch over you as men who must give an account. Obey them so that their work will be a joy, not a burden, for that would be of no advantage to you. (Hebrews 13:17)

The Point

All of this material from the Bible brings us to the point: there's a war going on, and you can't afford to sit by and watch any longer. God (as well as a large part of his Church) is busy fighting our enemies. We have God's Mission fully described in the Bible, the strategy and tactics to carry out that Mission, the fellow soldiers to march with, a well-identified enemy, a special system of training and discipline to get us ready for this kind of warfare, and the orders of the Commander himself to *get going*.

SELF-PREPARATION

The demands of the job are unique. The future church leader has to be master of himself, of the Word, and qualified to lead others in a focused effort to fulfill the Mission.

SELF-PREPARATION

There are two ways to meet the future: do nothing, or get ready for it. Obviously the only reason you will get ready for the future is if you realize that it will make demands on you that you are not prepared for now. That's the realistic view of the future. Many, however, think that they will be able to handle whatever the future holds without any preparation; but they are going to be surprised when they can't unravel the complex, unexpected problems that the ministry throws at them, in the short time that they have to solve them.

In class we learn the principles of warfare; in the world, we have chaotic situations to solve. The key to survival and success is to realize that we need to learn those principles of the Kingdom well ahead of time, so that we can *recognize* the principles in the chaos of life. It takes a mastery of your subject, and well-developed skills, before you can successfully apply those principles to the always-changing and unpredictable circumstances of life as they come at you. You can't predict exactly what the problems will be, or the solutions that you will use in your work; but you *can* be ready for whatever happens.

> Do your best to present yourself to God as one approved, a workman who does not need to be ashamed and who correctly handles the Word of truth. (2 Timothy 2:15)

What follows are the kinds of skills that you will need for the rigorous requirements of ministry in God's Kingdom.

Self-Discipline

Military training for leaders is different than the training for the regular recruits. The leaders have to show a higher level of self-drive, responsibility, and creative thinking. You will be leading and motivating church members to take God more seriously, and grow

Self-Preparation

spiritually – but nobody will be doing the same for you; you have to discipline yourself. And self-discipline is one of the hardest things to learn for most people who are used to being led. You have to focus on what is important, what is necessary, and keep at it; you will often have to deliberately set aside your other interests and pleasures for the sake of the well-being of the church. When others are relaxing, you are still working.

> **God-centered discipline** – The most important discipline to master concerns the very heart of our Christian faith: you must be God-centered. God has to become the center of your life. Unfortunately, it's not easy to do this. Even in the church, people have such a man-centered view of life that they think they can get along quite well without God.
>
>> For from him and through him and to him are all things. To him be the glory forever! Amen. (Romans 11:36)
>
>> What is more, I consider everything a loss compared to the surpassing greatness of knowing Christ Jesus my Lord, for whose sake I have lost all things. I consider them rubbish, that I may gain Christ and be found in him, not having a righteousness of my own that comes from the Law, but that which is through faith in Christ – the righteousness that comes from God and is by faith. I want to know Christ and the power of his resurrection and the fellowship of sharing in his sufferings, becoming like him in his death, and so, somehow, to attain to the resurrection from the dead. (Philippians 3:8-11)
>
> Holiness is when God is the center of our lives. We see and know him, we love what we see, we depend on and wait for his presence and power, and he guides us every step of the way. His wisdom is precious to us, and our constant study. His power is sufficient for all of our needs. We live only to serve and please him; our desire is to know him more fully, to stand in awe of his majesty and glory. Nothing else compares with God.

Self-Preparation

You have to master the knowledge of God. You have to learn his ways, his works, his Names, his Temple, his Law and requirements. In fact, the Bible will become for you *the revelation of God*, from beginning to end. It has no other purpose. It must become a textbook – *the* textbook for the Christian to master.

The leader has to have this attitude toward God because he is going to counsel others to come to this God for *their* needs. The leader must have personal experience in living with God in order to commend God's ways and works to others in need of help. You must discover personally, in your own life, just how much you need God – so that you can then pass on this knowledge to others. Your job in the ministry is to bring people to this God that you know, so they will get what you have received.

> Praise be to the God and Father of our Lord Jesus Christ, the Father of compassion and the God of all comfort, who comforts us in all our troubles, so that we can comfort those in any trouble with the comfort we ourselves have received from God. (2 Corinthians 1:3-4)

It is time to become like Enoch: he walked with God. (Genesis 5:24) Your calling is nothing less than that, nothing other than that.

Prayer – Prayer is communication between God and man. This too is difficult, for many reasons. For one thing, a very physical creature is attempting to understand and contact God who is spirit!

Another problem is that we tend to ask God for things we don't really need, and we ignore the things that God told us to focus on because we don't think we need them. Prayer is one of the least practiced of Christian functions, and the lack of answers from God shows how unskillful we are at it; he isn't much interested in our misguided prayers.

A lot has to be learned about the purpose and goal of prayer before you will become an effective "prayer warrior." For example, David understood the heart of God and what it would take to build God's Kingdom in God's way. He implemented five policies as requirements for the leaders of Israel to maintain after him, and passed on a prosperous and spiritually healthy nation to his son Solomon. David prayed about these issues continually; you will find him going back to them over and over in the Psalms. In the same way, these same priorities have to become your priorities; the Lord wants to hear you praying about his Kingdom before he will be interested in what you have to say. We will look more into these issues later.

Prayer also requires the kind of attitude that pleases God; he will refuse to answer the requests of the self-sufficient, the proud, the wicked, the materialistic, and the ignorant. The *way* you come to God greatly affects the outcome of prayer; he answers us according to our attitude. For example, he expects us to –

Pray according to his Word

> *Do good to your servant according to your Word, O LORD. (Psalm 119:65)*

The Bible is God's revelation to us about what's important to him; we show that we are in accord with his thoughts when we talk about those Kingdom issues with him.

Pray in his Name

> *I tell you the truth, my Father will give you whatever you ask in my name. (John 16:23)*

The Name of God actually opens doors into God's House; it identifies the God we want to talk to. Very simply, he answers when we call on him by Name.

Pray in the Spirit

> *And pray in the Spirit on all occasions with all kinds of prayers and requests. (Ephesians 6:18)*

Only the Spirit can lift us up into the presence of God so that we can see, hear him, understand him and worship him.

Pray with faith

> *But when he asks, he must believe and not doubt, because he who doubts is like a wave of the sea, blown and tossed by the wind. (James 1:6)*

Faith is living in God's spiritual world. In prayer we focus on the spiritual treasures that he has promised us; we understand and long for what we see spiritually.

Pray in line with his will

> *Your kingdom come, your will be done on earth as it is in heaven. (Matthew 6:10)*

There is only one will in God's Kingdom – his. Prayer is not telling him what to do, but getting orders from the King.

Pray for his glory

> *For from him and through him and to him are all things. To him be the glory forever! Amen. (Romans 11:36)*

The reason God made us (as well as everything else in Creation) is to glorify himself. Our goal is to glorify him in all that we do and say; so prayer is seeking the opportunity to do that.

In other words, the goal is to pray like a spiritual adult, not like a spiritual infant. You have to know what is on the heart of God, and forget your own agenda. You must have the matters of the Kingdom on your heart; those are the issues that great prayer warriors plead for from the throne of grace. And God wants to

Self-Preparation

see willing workers: instead of coming to these issues reluctantly, you come eager to get to work.[3]

Study – Learning is a life-long process; it's a way of life, a habitual mental discipline. It reflects a passion to know the truth, for self-improvement and becoming more useful to others. And it reflects maturity of character – the willingness to face one's mistakes, to change, and to improve.

Not only will you need to study the Bible, you will have to study people and situations, do research, always be on the lookout for opportunities and dangers, come up with creative solutions, and so on. Not only is the mental exercise good for you, but this discipline will prepare you with solutions for future problems, both your own and others.

Would-be officers typically spend two to three years studying on a college level before taking command of troops. The disciples spent three years studying with Jesus; Paul spent years in the wilderness before starting out on his great ministry. The reason is that there is much more to ministry than most people are aware of.

The Old Testament, in particular, is the sourcebook of Christian doctrine that the New Testament is based upon; you can't understand one without the other. So, you must become a master of the Book if you are going to teach it correctly.

First, the Bible must become your life-long study, the textbook on matters pertaining to God and man. And your attitude toward God's Word is crucial here: it's not your place to doubt it, or select only the parts that please you, or let the world's wisdom dictate to you how to handle it. Like a child, you must consider the Bible as nothing less than the truth from God – the only truth you will need in your ministry. Every word, phrase and idea is crucial for your success in the ministry and the life of the church. It will take all the energy and time that you have to master it, because it runs as deep as you are willing and able to go with it.

---

[3] For more on this subject, see the author's ***The Secret to Answered Prayer***.

> Man does not live on bread alone, but on every word
> that comes from the mouth of God. (Matthew 4:4)

Second, you must always be in learning mode – with everything in life, not just with the Bible – so that you can benefit from anything and everything that comes your way. There is so much to learn; not only are there new things to learn, but one of the most fruitful, and yet painful, sources of lessons is the problems that we have had. Unfortunately many quit learning after their formal years in school, and they end up running into unsolvable problems later in life – and yet they refuse to learn from their mistakes. Only a fool will refuse to learn from his experiences; he will stupidly hit that brick wall of a problem over and over without a clue of how to fix the problem.

> A rebuke impresses a man of discernment more
> than a hundred lashes a fool. (Proverbs 17:10)

The wise man studies everything and learns from it, so that he can improve and correct his course for future success. Study your own performance – to fine-tune it, to correct it, to learn from your mistakes and successes. Study your weaknesses; "examine yourselves to see whether you are in the faith; test yourselves." (2 Corinthians 13:5) Study the enemy and his ways of waging war. Study mankind in general; they are your future patients and students.

Dealing with the enemy – Every Christian is a warrior; so, you also have to learn war to win your own personal spiritual battles.

Paul has a lot to say about the importance of church leaders learning the principles of Christianity first before they purport to teach others.

> Everyone who competes in the games goes into strict training. They do it to get a crown that will not last; but we do it to get a crown that will last forever. Therefore I do not run like a man running aimlessly; I do not fight like a man beating the air. No, I beat my body and make it my slave so that after I have preached to others,

Self-Preparation

I myself will not be disqualified for the prize. (1 Corinthians 9:25-27)

Be diligent in these matters; give yourself wholly to them, so that everyone may see your progress. Watch your life and doctrine closely. Persevere in them, because if you do, you will save both yourself and your hearers. (1 Timothy 4:15-16)

Now the overseer must be above reproach, the husband of but one wife, temperate, self-controlled, respectable, hospitable, able to teach, not given to drunkenness, not violent but gentle, not quarrelsome, not a lover of money. He must manage his own family well and see that his children obey him with proper respect. (If anyone does not know how to manage his own family, how can he take care of God's church?) He must not be a recent convert, or he may become conceited and fall under the same judgment as the devil. He must also have a good reputation with outsiders, so that he will not fall into disgrace and into the devil's trap. (1 Timothy 3:2-7)

You, the leader, have to learn how to fight temptation, how to love righteousness and a "good reputation," how to work hard for God and others and not to be lazy, how to apply yourself to studying the Word and learning its precepts. You have to be willing to change and conform to Christ's expectations of you. You have to become more humble, more loving, more persevering, more patient and longsuffering, more courageous against the enemy.

You are an example of the point of Christianity: Christ's goal is to transform a sinner into a saint, not part of this world but getting ready to live in the next world with a holy God. It's especially important that you don't become a casualty yourself and fall to the enemy; it's fatal to one's ministry when you suffer from character issues, ignorance, lack of preparation, unholy alliances, a lack of spiritual resources, and a coolness to the things of God.

Self-Preparation

> Some have rejected these and so have shipwrecked their faith. Among them are Hymenaeus and Alexander, whom I have handed over to Satan to be taught not to blaspheme. (1 Timothy 1:19-20)

Good leaders lead from the front, not from the rear. In other words, they call others to follow their examples and do what they do. They *live* what they teach so that their followers will have not only words but actions to study. They do as Paul did:

> Follow my example, as I follow the example of Christ. (1 Corinthians 11:1)

> Don't let anyone look down on you because you are young, but set an example for the believers in speech, in life, in love, in faith and in purity. (1 Timothy 4:12)

Perseverance in trouble – Since a large part of ministry is dealing with a series of problems and trials (yours and others), you will have to be able to handle trouble. That's why the troops need a leader: he is someone with the wisdom and experience to solve problems and help the team achieve the Mission.

The most important thing is to keep your emotions under control; you have to keep a clear head under fire. If you are prone to panic and fear when faced with overwhelming problems, you aren't ready for leadership yet. If you plunge into depression when faced with unsolvable problems, your despair clouds your thinking and you are not able to persevere and study to find a solution.

> A man of knowledge uses words with restraint, and a man of understanding is even-tempered. (Proverbs 17:27)

> All his days he eats in darkness, with great frustration, affliction and anger. (Ecclesiastes 5:17)

You can tell if you are not able to handle the troubles and problems of leadership if you react to them in anger, frustration and impatience; if you are harsh toward others and too willing to

Self-Preparation

fight them; if you give up easily in the face of problems without answers. When even the little things of life throw you into these fits, it's doubtful that you can handle the burden of leadership – because it's a series of much more serious problems than daily irritations. And for leaders, the problems never quit coming.

Mastery of the Bible

If you haven't found this out already, let me tell you the bad news: Bible colleges and seminaries don't give you a command of the Bible. You would think that there is precisely where you would go to learn the Bible, but actually you won't. Bible schools focus more on the peripherals instead of the core course.

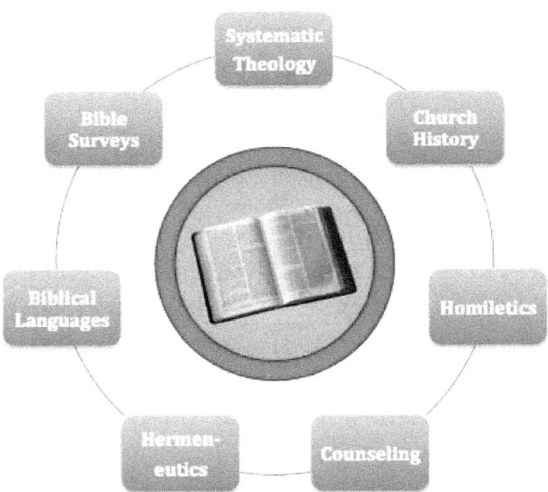

Peripherals with no core

Like all other institutions of higher learning, you will get overviews of many subjects (using the "fire-hose" technique of teaching: too much to learn, too short a time to learn it) and you will forget most of what you learned there by the time you graduate. Plus, their programs are designed to give you only an overview of the Bible.

Self-Preparation

The "peripherals" are good for leaders to learn, but that's not what you will use to feed the sheep back home. Probably 95% of what you learned in seminary has nothing to do with what you will teach them. You have to give them God's Word – as it stands, pure and simple. Yet you will get little in school on the Bible itself beyond simple and quick "Bible surveys". The result is that you will probably teach moralistic sermons instead of lessons on God.

So you will have to plumb the Bible's depths on your own.

The Bible is the Revelation of God – Whenever you sit down to the Bible, prepare to look for God in it. That is its only purpose. It has a lot to say about man, and some about the world, but its aim is to pull away the veil to show you God's nature and glory and works and ways. Here we walk into the Temple and see the true God.

So many people use the Bible for moralisms. They sound very holy and righteous, but they focus on man instead of God. "Believe in Jesus!" "Be holy!" "Live by faith!" "Be good!" On and on the moral lessons go in ignorant ministries. The fatal flaw in all of this is that *we can't do anything to save ourselves*. It's misleading – it's actually criminal – to make people believe that this is what Christianity is. Christianity is founded on what God does for us, not on what we do for him.

> Great are the works of the LORD; they are pondered
> by all who delight in them. (Psalm 111:2)

Biblical ministry focuses on God, not on man. If you want people to believe in Jesus, then teach them something about Jesus to believe in! Put content in that message. If you want them to be good, then show them the holy God who hates sin, commanded the Law, recreates the heart to conform to the standards of the Law, fills us with the Spirit to lead us in Christ's righteousness, and fills us with the fruit of the Spirit of Christ. Make God the actor, the grammatical subject of every sentence – not the constant object of *our* actions.

Self-Preparation

> For from him and through him and to him are all things. (Romans 11:36)

Themes – There are grand, over-arching themes of the Bible that make plain the message of God's Word and provide a skeleton into which everything in the Book fits. These are the *important* points to learn from the Bible. Start with these, and everything else will fall into the right place. If you get nothing else done in your ministry, you must master these themes and teach them to others.

Learn these themes well. They will guide you in what you must teach God's people, if you really want to show them the true meaning of the Word. There are many interesting things in the Bible, so much so that the average person can get lost amidst the details; you will have to help him sort out the most important themes and save the less important till later. As he grows, he first needs the "pure milk of the Word." Then he will need to learn the "fundamentals" of the faith. Finally he can get into the "deeper truths" of the faith and see the bigger picture of the Bible. All this guided study requires a good grasp of the basics of the Bible on your part.

> Like newborn babies, *crave pure spiritual milk*, so that by it you may grow up in your salvation, now that you have tasted that the Lord is good. (1 Peter 2:2-3)

> Therefore let us leave the elementary teachings about Christ and go on to *maturity*, not laying again the foundation of repentance from acts that lead to death, and of faith in God, instruction about baptisms, the laying on of hands, the resurrection of the dead, and eternal judgment. (Hebrews 6:1-2)

> They must keep hold of the *deep truths* of the faith with a clear conscience. (1 Peter 3:9)

These themes will also provide standards for your own studies. Make sure that everything you learn in the Bible fits in with the main themes of the Bible, or at least that they won't contradict

Self-Preparation

them. God doesn't contradict himself, and he's only got one message in the Bible. If you think that a passage teaches something that doesn't fit in with the plain teaching of the rest of the Bible, count on it – you have got it wrong. Keep studying until you see how it all fits together. God's Word is deeper than you think.[4]

OT & NT – Both sides of the Bible are important. People make a mistake when they set one side against another. There is *one* message in the Bible, and it's not Law versus Gospel! On the contrary, the Law is in the New Testament, and the Gospel is in the Old Testament. You must learn the purpose of each half of the Bible, so that you can benefit from both and not misuse either.

In brief: the *Old Testament* reveals Christ to us, in his many facets, and our relationship that we have with God through him. The *New Testament* shows us the New Man, and how we can become one with him. Both reveal the way of salvation in Christ; the Old looks forward to the event, and the New relies on the Old for its doctrinal explanation of the event.[5]

There is so much to work on here. The Apostles were masters of the Old Testament, so that they would preach the *correct* Gospel about Christ. Study their Gospel sermons in Acts and you will see them using sermon points that focus on Old Testament themes – not whatever modern trends that church members like to hear about.[6]

> But as for you, continue in what you have learned and have become convinced of, because you know those from whom you learned it, and how from infancy you have known the holy Scriptures *[that is, the Old Testament]*, which are able to make you wise for

---

[4] For more on this, see the author's **Eight Fundamentals of the Christian Faith** and **Ten Keys to the Bible**.

[5] See the author's *A New Model For Biblical Studies* and **Where the Paths Meet**.

[6] See the author's **The Gospel of Christ** for more information on what the Apostles taught about Christ.

salvation through faith in Christ Jesus. (2 Timothy 3:14-15)

And we are obligated to preach their Gospel the way they passed it on to us.

> I praise you for remembering me in everything and for holding to the teachings, just as I passed them on to you. (1 Corinthians 11:2)

> So then, brothers, stand firm and hold to the teachings we passed on to you, whether by word of mouth or by letter. (2 Thessalonians 2:15)

Principles of the church – The church is the only agency on earth that can address man's spiritual needs, because it uses principles forged in Israel's history. And Jesus faithfully brings those principles into the ministry of the Church. But modern church leaders don't seem to appreciate how critical it is to follow Christ's lead here. They are instead basing the church on modern cultural principles: entertainment, psychological self-help, consumer-driven programs, successful business methods, salesmanship, current events, etc.

For example, Christ's church can only survive if it has a clear *Mission statement*:

- Our Mission is to be saved from our sins.
- Our Mission is to get ready to live with God in Heaven forever.

> You were taught, with regard to your former way of life, to put off your old self, which is being corrupted by its deceitful desires; to be made new in the attitude of your minds; and to put on the new self, created to be like God in true righteousness and holiness. (Ephesians 4:22-24)

We will elaborate more on this Mission later.

Self-Preparation

You must also have *five pillars* of operations in your church if you hope to achieve this Mission; it's not going to happen on its own without the proper church support system in place. David first worked out these principles as he put the nation of Israel back together, in conformity to God's standards for a righteous Kingdom. The Church too must follow his model; as we read the story of Jesus in the Gospels, so much of what he did makes sense when seen against the backdrop of David's five-point plan. This is, of course, why they called him "the Son of David"!

- David set up his capital in Jerusalem, and from there ruled over his Kingdom. Jesus set up his capital in Heaven. Location is everything, as the saying goes; by basing his Kingdom in Heaven, Jesus is focusing our attention on a *spiritual* Kingdom, the Heavenly Jerusalem; and he wants us to set our goal on the spiritual treasures that he gives us from there. He's not interested in an earthly kingdom.

- David summarily dealt a decisive blow against the enemies of Israel, long a thorn in their side. So does Jesus – he came to destroy the world, the flesh and the devil. We simply can't live at peace and grow spiritually if we have forces continually harassing us and preventing us from reaching our objective. So we are called to fight our enemies with the weapons and tactics that Jesus gives us.

- David's job included bringing the Israelites back to the God who first called them to be his people; it was time to get rid of their idols of false gods, and learn to live with God in close communion. And Jesus came for the same reason: that we might know God, live with him, grow in the knowledge of God, trust him and follow him, and glorify him. God must become central to our minds and hearts.

- David set up a government through which he could rule over the entire nation, executing the will of God at all levels of society. Jesus sets up his government

Self-Preparation

> in the Church and gives them the task of implementing his will, and building his Kingdom. We must take our place in the hierarchy of Christ's Kingdom: he is Lord, we submit to his authority, and we follow his officers whom he put over us to lead us to Heaven.
>
> - David wrote down the plans for the Temple to be built in Jerusalem (given to him by the Spirit) and passed those plans to his son Solomon to actually build it. Jesus too is building a Temple of which we are a part – in fact, Christians are the living stones of the house of God. We are part of God's Temple now: we are all priests with responsibilities and duties toward God and man.

Almost no church in our day has all five pillars in place; therefore they *will* fail at some point, someday. They don't have a complete system to address any and every problem that may come up; there are weaknesses in their defenses. But the church that is careful to build on that foundation of the Mission, and erect these five pillars of church operations, will have what they need to weather any storm and get its members to their objective. [7]

As a leader, you will have to know Christ's program so instinctively that you can keep the entire church on track and moving forward to its goal, and ruthlessly eliminate anything that interferes with, or doesn't add to, the Mission.

Teaching skills – The primary function of the leader is to teach God's people. It's not accidental that so many of the gifts of the Spirit center around the transmission of the Word of God – from teachers to learners:

> It was he who gave some to be Apostles, some to be Prophets, some to be evangelists, and some to be pastors and teachers, to prepare God's people for works of service, so that the body of Christ may be built up

---

[7] For more on this, see the author's ***The Throne of David***.

Self-Preparation

until we all reach unity in the faith and in the knowledge of the Son of God and become mature, attaining to the whole measure of the fullness of Christ. (Ephesians 4:11-13)

As many new teachers have found out, it can be very difficult to stand before a group of people and teach a coherent lesson that everyone can follow and learn from. It takes skill and practice to teach God's Word. You must know the right things to focus on; so much teaching in the Church consists of rabbit-trails that aren't of any benefit for people's spiritual walk. You must know how to make it "short and sweet" – just enough for a lesson, and very memorable and usable for the busy church member. Qualified teachers have usually taken years to get to their level of expertise.

An axiom in teaching circles is that the teacher must know ten times as much of the subject as he intends to teach to his students. This gives him a wide scope of knowledge to give him confidence in his subject, to answer questions, to know the right emphasis to make, and to avoid saying the wrong things.

> Therefore every teacher of the Law who has been instructed about the Kingdom of Heaven is like the owner of a house who brings out of his storeroom new treasures as well as old. (Matthew 13:52)

And it's another axiom that your students will remember no more than 10% of what they hear, 50% of what they see, and 90% of what they do themselves. This means that effective teaching requires skills to engage the student on several levels if you want the lesson to stick.

Self-Preparation

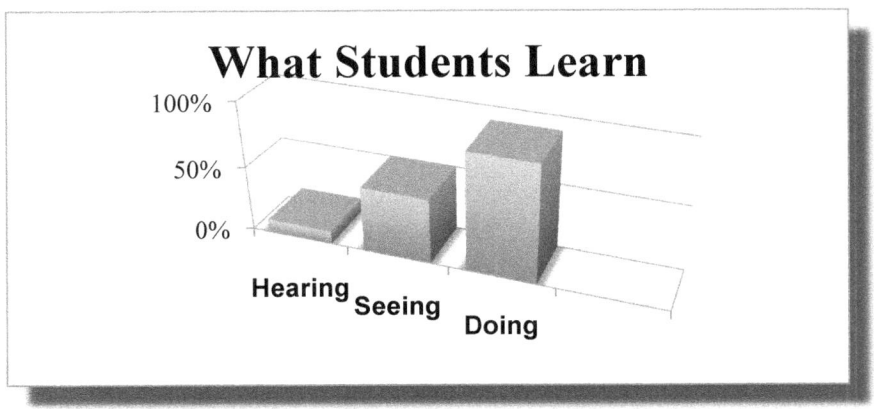

Learn human nature

Your job as the leader is to home in on what people really need spiritually. What is it in the human heart and mind that needs fixing? What is the problem? What is the antidote? What makes people resist the very thing that will help them? How best should it be applied? What is the goal, in other words, that we are aiming at for a Christian to be saved? And how do we get there?

Study the heart – You must become a student of the heart. People act according to the way they feel and think; Jesus said that we can know what people are like by what comes out of their hearts. So, God's spiritual solutions are aimed at specific problem areas: the goal is to identify what motivates people, change their motivations and goals, and then steer them towards God. All the while our job is made more difficult by the fact that so many people are hypocritical; they hide their true feelings behind a façade of a nice personality.

You have to understand the scope and damage of sin, the weaknesses of the heart that make it so prone to follow temptations of the world, the mental makeup that makes people believe lies instead of the truth. You must become a doctor of the soul: you have to correctly diagnose the spiritual sickness that someone is suffering under, and be willing to confront that sickness with God's answers. And these insights will come to

Self-Preparation

you only if you are very familiar with Biblical principles. We need God's perspective on things here, not man's.

Listening is a rare skill, especially among leaders (unfortunately!). But you will have to learn to listen and quit talking so much.

> Guard your steps when you go to the house of God. Go near to listen rather than to offer the sacrifice of fools, who do not know that they do wrong. Do not be quick with your mouth, do not be hasty in your heart to utter anything before God. God is in heaven and you are on earth, so let your words be few. As a dream comes when there are many cares, so the speech of a fool when there are many words. (Ecclesiastes 5:1-3)

Everyone has an opinion, and most of us delight in making our opinions known. The result is that we usually don't know what other people think, or what they are going through, unless they are just as pushy about their opinions as we are! A leader has to be different if he is going to get anywhere with his followers, however. Listening enables him to identify all the elements of a situation, assess the strengths and weaknesses of everyone involved, and pick up any clues that he might need to solve the problems.

The book of Proverbs will help you tremendously in this area. Here is a wide range of case studies that analyze the human heart and what must be done to correct its ills.

> Understanding is a fountain of life to those who have it, but folly brings punishment to fools. (Proverbs 16:22)

Tap into spiritual resources – The Lord has given the Church exactly what people need to know God and change from sinner to saint. The treasures of Heaven are like medicines, and surgical procedures, for our spiritual illnesses. Since we have such a wide range of problems that no single solution will meet the requirements of all, it's your job to know the solutions and what will work in each situation. *You* are the skilled doctor.

Self-Preparation

So many ministries take a shallow approach to the problems of church members, giving them the "gospel" every Sunday – which means that they tell them to "believe in Jesus" over and over. But just like physical growth, the Christian requires more depth, more complex answers, and more mature solutions to his growing spiritual needs. Otherwise he will remain a spiritual infant all of his life. The leader has to grade his material according to the changing needs of his students.

This means, of course, that he also must grow himself and learn to use these treasures in his own spiritual life.

> Praise be to the God and Father of our Lord Jesus Christ, the Father of compassion and the God of all comfort, who comforts us in all our troubles, so that we can comfort those in any trouble with the comfort we ourselves have received from God. For just as the sufferings of Christ flow over into our lives, so also through Christ our comfort overflows. If we are distressed, it is for your comfort and salvation; if we are comforted, it is for your comfort, which produces in you patient endurance of the same sufferings we suffer. (2 Corinthians 1:3-6)

Learn war

Life is not a game; it's a war, and people are dying every day at the hand of the enemy. You as a church leader are specially called to engage this terrible enemy, and apply sound military principles to bring down his strongholds. You must also train your church members in the science of offense and defense so that they can survive the war. It's part of your job to learn war.

> Praise be to the LORD my Rock, who trains my hands
> for war, my fingers for battle. (Psalm 144:1)

Assessment of situations – One of the most important skills of a leader is to be able to size up a situation and understand exactly what's going on, and what it will take to win a battle. In military parlance this skill is called "coup d'oeil" (*koo-dwah*)– literally, the "glance of the eye." Many a leader have misjudged people and circumstances, applying solutions that don't fit and leading the group into chaos and disaster. Since problems often come thick and fast, you will have to think on your feet and come up with the *right* solutions quickly. This ability does not come naturally for most people; you have to practice.

You are going to have people coming to you with baggage in their lives, both visible and hidden. You will have to not only truly assess *where they are* spiritually, but also discern *what they will need*. Some people are sheep, some are wolves; can you tell the difference in time before someone hurts the church? Some people need encouragement, some need rebuke, some need extended training and some are future leaders. As the leader, you are the only one in the church who can direct each to their particular solutions.

Leadership is learned in times of peace, when the demands are light and you have an opportunity for study. Learn from the masters of the past and how they solved their problems; learn from their failures as well as their successes. Learn from the Kings in the Old Testament as some successfully maintained David's Kingdom and some did not. Learn Jesus' solutions as he assesses the Pharisees and instructs his disciples. Practice by studying churches and ministries and applying the principles that you are learning. Imagine yourself in their shoes – what would you do in their situation?

Napoleon prepared for his battles *three months* before they happened; he went over the details so many times, covering all the possibilities in his mind first, that the result was repeated successes on the battlefield. Nothing surprised him; he had a ready solution for every possible problem.

Principles of warfare – There are two ways of doing ministry: ignorantly and wisely. The wise will recognize that God gave us powerful principles to work from to insure success in this spiritual war that we are in.

Self-Preparation

The Old Testament gives us amazingly relevant and powerful rules of warfare for Christian ministry. So many people stumble over the military aspect of the Old Testament, thinking that it's an ancient relic of bloodthirsty primitives that we peace-loving Christians can safely ignore. *Wrong!* The Old Testament is a study in military strategy and tactics that we must use against our present enemies. It's a textbook on spiritual warfare. For example, we learn how to identify the enemy, follow God's leading into battle, and be ruthless against the enemy. If you fight the world, the flesh and the devil in the same way that God instructed the Israelites to fight their enemies, you will win every time. Ignore this material, and you will lose. These are God-given principles for war in our day.

Strategies & Tactics – *Strategy* covers the purpose of the war (or the Mission), correctly identifying the enemy, the theater of operations, logistics and fortifications. *Tactics* covers the maneuvers and methods used in the actual fighting. The average soldier knows almost nothing of strategy, and very little of tactics – he doesn't need to be an expert in either. He simply follows orders and shoots at the enemy. But leaders have to have this broader view of things; they move around whole armies and battalions on the battlefield while the individual soldier uses his gun.

You have to understand the Mission of the church and keep the members on track. You have the needs of the entire group in mind, while members are basically thinking of themselves for the most part. You have to decide where and when to fight, and keep the enemy from deciding those for you. You have to identify the skills and spiritual gifts in the group and put them in the places where they will be of the most effect. You have to turn the group towards the enemy and encourage them to keep fighting as long as the enemy fights. Your viewpoint, in other words, is larger than the individual members' viewpoint; you as a leader have to think on that higher level.

Paul, for example, was always thinking on a strategic as well as a tactical level. His letters to the churches reflect his deep analysis

Self-Preparation

of their situations. And he was also surveying the larger sphere of operations as he moved throughout the Roman Empire to build and visit churches from one end to the other.

Leadership principles & character – It takes a different level of skills and character to be a leader. Lots of people would love to be a leader because they want to be in charge; but leadership requires the ability to study, an extraordinary ability to persevere and keep the Mission in view through all obstacles, the skill and determination to apply the principles of warfare unflinchingly to the end, and above all a thick skin to criticism and rebellion.

Leaders have to know the principles of warfare on the level of instinct. During battle, chaos and confusion usually rule – to the extent that a poorly trained leader will have no idea what to do, or he will do the wrong thing and be soundly defeated. It doesn't take genius to win; it takes a lot of study beforehand. Defeat almost always comes as a result of poor planning and training, of not being able to see the clear principles of the classroom out on the field of battle.

The Lord's Mission – Let's repeat how important it is to understand the Mission. In the military, there's a difference between training and the Mission. Training gets you ready for battle conditions of any sort. The Mission, however, is the objective that the Commander-in-Chief gives his officers on the eve of battle when they are trained and ready to fight.

The Mission is a clearly stated, simple-to-understand description of what the Commander-in-Chief wants us to achieve. We have described this Mission already to some degree. The important thing to grasp is that *everyone* must understand this Mission, from the highest officers to the lowest ranks. Everything we do must directly support and achieve this Mission; whatever we are doing that doesn't directly support this Mission is excess baggage and must be set aside. The army that hones its skills and gathers together the equipment and supplies that will enable them to achieve this Mission will never lose; it is focused and strong, ready for battle.

Self-Preparation

Bible examples – Again we must repeat that the Bible is a textbook for spiritual warfare. You would do well to study the battles and leaders of the Bible, in both the Old and New Testaments.

Study both successes and failures. Not everyone in the Bible understood how to defeat the enemy; there were always losses and casualties in the Lord's army. The great commanders of the faith knew how to rely on God's treasures, and use his methods, in their battles of faith. Moses, Joshua, David, Hezekiah, Nehemiah, Jesus, and Paul are just a few of the success stories. The losses also are instructive: many of the Judges, the kings of Israel and Judah, Judas, the Pharisees, even some of the Apostles like Peter in his weak moments and ignorance.

Don't stumble over the physical nature of the battles of the Old Testament. The *principles* are the same; the Church must do battle in the same way against its spiritual enemies.

In summary, these are the kinds of topics that will be covered in the following chapters.

Wider studies

History – It's a common saying that those who don't study history are doomed to repeat it. In other words, as Ecclesiastes tells us, "There is nothing new under the sun." Everything that you will face has been dealt with by others before you, in some way and in some place. The names have changed, but the principles have not. Learn from them!

Study church history; you would be amazed at what has happened in churches in the past over and over again, and even more amazed at the creative and effective ways that Christians have dealt with these issues that you are facing now.

Study the world's history to get a deeper picture of the heart of man, the scope of sin, the need for salvation, the political and social and business and educational issues that inevitably have their roots in the moral and spiritual realm. The very root of

Self-Preparation

history, the thing that actually generates what we call "history," is an individual's response to a test that God brings into their lives. There is a lot of instructive material here for the student of the heart.

Biographies – This is a specialized form of history, and very profitable for the church leader. Napoleon said that the military leader will best learn the art of war by studying the great commanders of history. They are a rich resource of problem-solving and methodology. The church has 2000 years of great leaders who have faced, and successfully dealt with, the problems of their age.

Theology – This area is more advanced than simple Bible studies. *Systematic theology* is actually an outline of our Christian doctrines, set forth clearly, and used as a concise and complete standard of what we believe. It's not a replacement of the Bible itself, but it's the summary statement of what we have learned from the Bible. It gives balance and fullness to our Christian faith.

Biblical theology focuses on themes that run throughout the Old and New Testaments and tie the entire Book into an organized whole. The Abrahamic Covenant, for example, forms the beginning of God's plan of salvation and culminates in the giving of the Spirit as Jesus fulfills that Covenant for Abraham's heirs in the Church.

Usually church denominations have their own theologies, because they understand the Bible in different ways from other denominations. Unfortunately these different points of view have caused war within the ranks of the Church instead of directing our efforts toward the real enemy. No theology is complete, simply because our understanding of God's Word can't be as comprehensive as the mind of God himself. Our attitude should be one of humility, ready to learn and change when necessary instead of fighting over the limited understanding we have of things. For this reason, one should study theology carefully, for the right purpose – as an aid to understanding the fullness and depth of the Bible, not as a replacement of it.

Heresies – One of the primary reasons we should study theology is so that we can identify heresies when we see them. A *heresy* is a deviation from the truth of God that leads us away from his saving grace. Ignorance isn't necessarily a heresy; but when someone deliberately leads us away from the method of salvation in Christ that God has given us, that's cause for discipline, and war if necessary.

The reason this is important is because the average church member doesn't know the truth well enough to spot a heresy when it raises its ugly head. That's why so many millions have left the church and joined cults. Lies are usually clothed with much truth to disguise themselves. The leader has to not only know the truth, but also be familiar with the standard heresies (the heresies we have now have actually been around for 2000 years in some form or another – there really is nothing new under the sun!). Like guardians of the gate, the church leaders make sure that heresies don't get a chance to spread among the members.

Why the military model?

What I've been describing here is using a military model for preparation and training for the ministry. There are a number of models that one can use when working in the church: community spokesman, counseling, compassion and grace, testimony and witness, educational. Each model can be used to address specific needs. The military model is not the only one to use, nor will it be the appropriate one to use every time.

But there are certain tasks that require the military model, because it answers those particular situations better than all the other models will. We will never achieve certain critical results in the church unless we shift our perspective; certain tasks in the church can only be seen and appreciated if one takes a military approach to it. For example, Paul uses it to teach us the importance of self-discipline.

> Endure hardship with us like a good soldier of Christ Jesus. No one serving as a soldier gets involved in civilian

Self-Preparation

affairs – he wants to please his commanding officer. (2 Timothy 2:3-4)

So, we must be ready to use whatever is necessary in the work of the church. Since we *are* at war, then it's the responsible thing to do to learn war.

All the elements that make a successful army are also necessities in the church if it wants to win its battles. The military model provides the best approach to the problem of war because:

- **It's methodical** – It's just a matter of applying tried-and-true principles over and over until everyone is skilled and ready for the job.

- **It hits the salient points** – Through reconnaissance, the necessary weapons, and focus, it hits the danger points and solves the problem immediately and effectively.

- **It builds awareness** – The military has to know what's going on around it so that the enemy won't take it by surprise.

- **It provides discipline** – Everyone has to work in unison, from top down, with no snags in authority or communication or obedience. Discipline is literally the key to victory.

- **It gives procedures** – There's a procedure for everything in the military. They've figured out ahead of time how to deal with problems and functions, and the best way to do it; everyone knows that if you follow this procedure, you will end up with the same results every time.

- **It builds preparedness** – Through constant training, and keeping the Mission in mind, the church is ready for any problem at any time. It can swing into action immediately.

Self-Preparation

Much of what has to happen in the Church depends on these advantages, which should therefore give us incentive to study the military model.

Above all, we need the military model because we truly are fighting against enemies. This is not a game that we are playing; we are in the middle of a ruthless and devastating war, and people are losing their souls by the thousands every day and headed for an eternity of misery and death. Our enemies will only give way before a ruthless response from us. The Commander of God's armies is determined to defeat these enemies and he calls us to fall in behind him and learn war.

The military has something that civilians don't have: they are *ready* for a fight. Civilians are undisciplined, and will run away in a panic in times of danger. When the enemy approaches, the military is your only answer – it has the necessary discipline, weaponry, skills, preparedness and leadership to defend the territory and beat back the enemy. And the secret is training and discipline beforehand, and courage in the battlefield. The military system requires time to put together, and a lot of wisdom and dedication. That's why we have to take this model seriously and make sure it's built into the daily operations of the church, along with all the other things that the church is responsible for.

ASSESSMENT OF THE POSITION

The leader has to be able to assess a new church job correctly. He has to see the situation clearly, the needs, the requirements, and the basic strategy required to meet the needs. Above all, he has to see whether the fight is winnable – or whether he should move on to another position.

ASSESSMENT OF THE POSITION

Whether the new leader is a first-time pastor or a seasoned warrior, he must take his job seriously. He has been specially called by the Commander-in-Chief to take on the task of leading the troops into spiritual battle. A particular job – be it a church pastorate, or a Sunday School class, or working in a para-church organization – demands particular skills that the Lord has, providentially and wisely, equipped this leader with. It's no accident that the right man shows up for the job.

On the other hand, all the good intentions in the world won't straighten out a mess that God never called us into. So many church programs start out with fanfare and great hopes, only to fail because they were works of man and not of God.

As we mentioned before, the good leader has what is called *coup d'oeil* – the ability to instantly size up a situation correctly. So many battles have been lost over the inability of an incompetent commander to see the situation for what it was. The question, therefore, for every person considering a ministry position is this: is this God's work that I'm considering, or man's work?

I once saw an advertisement for a pastor of a church. Among other things, the church listed 50 plus items that they required from this new pastor – most of which were not from the Bible! A person would be a fool to take a job like that. If he didn't actually descend to the level of an abject employee satisfying the whims of demanding consumers, he would be in a constant battle with his own congregation making ridiculous demands on him. The Mission would never get done; he would be too busy catering to their non-Biblical agenda.

In contrast, the Apostles in the book of Acts correctly cleared the stage for their own ministry by assigning deacons to the tasks of the physical needs of the church – so that they could do what they were called to do:

So the Twelve gathered all the disciples together and said, "It would not be right for us to neglect the ministry of the Word of God in order to wait on tables. Brothers, choose seven men from among you who are known to be full of the Spirit and wisdom. We will turn this responsibility over to them and will give our attention to ***prayer*** and the ***ministry of the Word***." (Acts 6:24)

If you ever see a job opening like this one, take it! It's the perfect setup for someone who is serious about achieving the Mission of the church.

Areas to examine

In order to find out what you need to know about a Christian group or church, here are the places to look. Every group has most if not all of these items, and they reveal a great deal about the nature of the group and what you will be up against.

- **Statement of faith** – Most churches and Christian organizations have a statement of faith. And most of them are acceptable on the surface. The problem is that they don't always tell you everything.

  The Apostles' Creed is most helpful here. If someone can say that they believe the concepts in that Creed, it usually means that they are orthodox and conservative in their faith, no matter what other secondary beliefs they may have. The very basics of Christianity focus on our idea of God, Jesus Christ, miracles, the Holy Spirit, the nature of the Church, and Judgment Day.

  Sometimes the group knows what the hot issues are in Christian circles and they will be right up front about them: like the version of the Bible they use, or their "rightly dividing" the Scriptures (*dispensationalism*), or their view on eschatology. But often you have to probe to find out the peculiar beliefs of the group. Once I spent about two hours questioning a particular group, trying to find out their beliefs. It finally came out after the right questions exposed their position – it turned out that they were Arian; they didn't believe that Jesus was the Son of God. How many people join groups like that and never suspect until it's too late that they are heretical in their beliefs?

Also, a statement of faith is often revealing about what it *doesn't* mention. I once saw a statement of faith for a conservative seminary – it said absolutely nothing about the Old Testament except for a mention of Creation. As if the Old Testament was not a rich source for Christian doctrine! That told me they were a "New Testament only" institution. I wouldn't be interested in a job there.

You will also want to examine the church "constitution", because often a church won't have a statement of faith *per se*. They include all the information about their church in their constitution. Legally a church is required to satisfy the requirements of the civil government as regarding nonprofit organizations; the constitution will address those issues. But often you will find the structure of the church government here also.

- **Job description** – As mentioned above, compare the job description with the requirements of the Bible. Sometimes it's ignorance that leads a congregation to pile on extra-curricular responsibilities for their pastors. But often they really do expect the poor man to cater to their every whim. You will have to find out which it is, and decide whether you can educate them into a more Biblical position on the leader's role there.

Your job is to instruct the people in the way of salvation, to help them see the way of life in Christ, to lead them out of this world and into the next one. If the church isn't looking for this in its pastor or elder, you

Assessment of the Position

will only have a continuous fight on your hands; you won't be able to do what the Lord expects of you.

> Until I come, devote yourself to the public reading of Scripture, to preaching and to teaching. Do not neglect your gift, which was given you through a prophetic message when the body of elders laid their hands on you. (1 Timothy 4:13-14)

- **Hierarchy** – One of the pillars of the church's ministry is a healthy awareness of the hierarchy of the church. Christ is the Head, we are the body. Man doesn't lead; Jesus does. This even extends to the government of the church: we do not submit the ministry and functions of the church to a democratic vote. Following this logic, we can see that the leader's role is not to decide what the church should be doing, but faithfully executing the Commander's will in the church. That's why his role centers so much around teaching the Word. It's a matter of everyone sitting at the feet of the pastor and teachers and learning God's will.

Of course this requires a healthy respect for leadership in the church. Probe their history a bit and you will discover their attitude toward those in leadership. If they follow their leaders, that's a good situation; if they tend to run every leader out of town on a rail over trivial matters, you may not survive their wrath either.

If, therefore, the government of the church consists of extreme democracy, where everyone (including the leaders) have a single vote and everyone leads in the meetings, then you would do well to look elsewhere for a place of ministry. It won't be the will of Christ that rules, but the will of man. But if the church has elders and deacons – which is, you will remember, the Lord's specific instructions for a church government – then you have a better chance of carrying out the Lord's will in that group.

> The reason I left you in Crete was that you might straighten out what was left unfinished and appoint elders in every town, as I directed you. (Titus 1:5)

- **Facilities** – The group has to have a place to meet that will accommodate its ministry goals. A living room is fine for a half-dozen people; but you need a bigger facility for a sizeable group. You also need free access to it for the group's meetings (someone else may own the facility you want, and they only make it available to you at very inconvenient times for your group). And you don't want the physical facilities to present a burden or obstacle to your spiritual program: in other words, don't saddle the church with such debt that it can't focus on the Mission.

Keep in mind that the churches in the days of the Apostles met in people's homes. They were glad to do it and the church thrived spiritually. The point isn't necessarily that we also must meet in homes; it's just that a viable church doesn't depend on multi-million dollar budgets and modern American facilities. The building should never be so big as to overshadow, or even prevent, the real work going on.

There are all sorts of aspects to consider when looking at the facilities. People can make do with many limitations, but some situations are just not going to work. I knew of a pastor who set up his church on Bourbon Street in New Orleans, right beside the brothels and bars. No doubt he was making a statement, but I doubt the wisdom of forcing believers (especially with families) to parade before strip joints and sleaze in order to worship God in "purity of mind and heart." In the end, he himself fell to the sins of the flesh and the church closed in disgrace. Pride drives people to overdo the physical aspects of church just as much as its spiritual aspects.

Assessment of the Position

- **Leadership** – Definitely try to get a measure on the existing leadership in the church. *First* of all, are these the kinds of leaders who will follow your lead? You will be making important changes, introducing new ideas, leading in new directions – will they follow you? Or are they going to rebel against you?

  Second, find out the kinds of things that they have been doing in the church. It may be that you will end up undoing much of their work. They may have laid rotten foundations that you will have to expend much time and energy to tear back out and replace.

  Third, are they strong enough in the church that, if you try to re-train them or (even worse) get rid of them, they would stir up the church against you? Often a person who has been a leader in a church for many years is much-loved, for good or bad reasons, and the group will usually turn to them instead of following a new leader (you) who is confronting them with uncomfortable issues.

If you can, spend time in these areas and do some serious reconnaissance work so that you can answer some important questions about your potential job assignment.

Questions to ask

Often we are so glad to land a job that the only question that we ask is "how much is the pay?" We think that as long as the situation looks fairly reasonable on the surface, we can handle whatever problems might come up.

This is so foolish. As proof that this isn't enough, the common statistic for seminary graduates is that they last about two years at their first pastorate, rarely any longer. The problem is that the church doesn't know what to look for, and the new graduate doesn't know why he's there. They like each other, he takes the job, and then the honeymoon shortly wears off as they discover painfully that they can't work with each other.

So it's wise to ask some pertinent questions *before* one leaps into the position.

1. *Is it good ground?*

Militarily speaking, this is one of the most profound questions that you can ask, and a sure sign that you know what you are doing. A commander would be a fool to fight on poor ground.

"Good ground" means that you will have the advantage over the enemy because of the position. You have the stronger position, you have freedom of movement, you can keep your eye on the enemy and he can't see you. You certainly don't want the enemy to have the good ground! And it takes a trained eye to be able to assess the position correctly; a mistake here will cost you the battle. Skilled commanders will usually avoid the fight if the conditions are against them.

These are the elements that make "good ground" for the fight.

- **Strong lines of operation** – The "line of operation" is your route back to your supplies, the line of safety in retreat, the route that your supply train and resources take to get to your position. Napoleon once said that any commander who lets his enemy cut that line of operation ought to be hung. That's especially true for the Christian: God is our resource; we desperately need the treasures of Heaven to fight this war. If we get cut off from that, we deserve a good thrashing from the enemy.

    > May the LORD answer you when you are in distress; may the name of the God of Jacob protect you. May he send you help from the sanctuary and grant you support from Zion. (Psalm 20:1-2)

Assessment of the Position

Our connection with God and the resources of Heaven come by way of prayer and the Word, and through the gifts of the Spirit operating in the Church. Above all else, you have to keep those lines of supply open and operating efficiently.

Every commander knows that the best way to defeat his enemy is to cut their supply line. And you have no doubt experienced that from the hands of your spiritual enemies: when prayer dried up, you felt alone and helpless, and God "no longer went out with your army." (Psalm 60:10) It's your own fault if you let yourself get in that position. When the Lord promises to "set our feet on the Rock," the only way we can account for our defeat in battle is if we moved away from him, not he from us!

> Remain in me, and I will remain in you. No branch can bear fruit by itself; it must remain in the vine. Neither can you bear fruit unless you remain in me. (John 15:4)

At the beginning, however, you will have to assess the situation and determine whether this group will make it impossible to keep those supply lines to Heaven open. Are they learners? Do they want to learn more? Do they take prayer seriously? Is church important to them? Are they willing to change and become more like Christ? If not, then (as the saying goes) you can lead a horse to water but you can't make him drink.

> And he did not do many miracles there because of their lack of faith. (Matthew 13:58)

- **Freedom of movement** – Above all things, you need the freedom to move and fight. If you are told right up front that there are certain things that you can't do – the church won't allow you to do those things – then you should reconsider whether you want this position. Churches, or the power players in a church, have often

Assessment of the Position

tried to tell the new pastor what he can preach and what he can't preach. It's a serious mistake to put shackles on his freedom of movement. "Shake the dust off your feet" and look for another place.

You as the leader have to have access to all the resources of the church, and you need to be able to do whatever it takes to achieve the Mission. Nobody should be telling you "that's not your job", not if it pertains to the life and health of the church. Everything is your responsibility; and if you aren't the person who will actually be doing the work, you will be assigning the right person to it and should expect an accounting from that person. From your vantage point as the leader, you can see things that others can't see, and you know the battle plan better than everyone else does. If you can't do the work (or have it done), who will?

I know of a church that told its new youth director to put off his planned Bible studies for a couple of years. The kids need "relationships" now, not Bible! That's not acceptable; if he can see that it's Bible that they really need, the church shouldn't be telling him otherwise.

- **Cannot be dominated** – Usually "good ground" includes the high places. Not only does it give you a better perspective to see what's going on, but it's much harder to struggle up the hill to your enemy than to fall down on him. Battles have been won and lost over the struggle for the high places.

  The "high place" in a church is the position of authority; it's the role of the leader. Unfortunately in most modern churches, the congregation styles itself as the employer, and it considers its pastor as its employee. He has to cater to *their* whims. This is a terrible situation for a pastor to be in. Moses was challenged by Korah and his followers, and God destroyed the rebels to demonstrate his choice of Moses

Assessment of the Position

as Israel's leader. Paul had to defend his right and calling as an Apostle with the authority to speak to the Corinthian church.

In spite of our modern democratic yet misguided notions, the role of a leader is critical for the group's success. He is usually the only one with the training and skills to identify the Mission and equip everyone to do the job. He understands the situation; he is self-disciplined and understands how important it is to keep everyone moving in the right direction. Many people would love to be the leader (in order to get the perks!) but very few are capable of leading others and succeeding at it.

The leader has a difficult job as it is. If the time comes for him to confront someone with their sin, or if he's attempting to lead the group to a new spiritual level, he can't do that if he keeps getting overruled by stubborn and ignorant church members. If their vote can stop him, then they dominate him; *they* are the leaders. But if they acknowledge that the Lord put this man in a position of authority over them, they will submit and follow even if they don't understand what he's doing – because they trust him, and because the Lord told them to obey him.

> Obey your leaders and submit to their authority. They keep watch over you as men who must give an account. Obey them so that their work will be a joy, not a burden, for that would be of no advantage to you. (Hebrews 13:17)

- **You can reach all areas** – During battle you will often need to move your troops or supplies into any and every area of the field of battle. The one thing you don't want are people or obstacles standing in your way. You can lose battles very quickly if you can't get somewhere fast enough to keep the enemy out.

In one church there was a women's group that was strictly off-limits to the leadership of the church. Not only did that lead to false teachings going on there which the church could do nothing about, the group led vicious campaigns against the leaders of the church whenever efforts were made to bring their "ministry" in line with the rest of the church. The upshot was that the church told the women's group that if they really wanted to be that separate, they needed to go somewhere else and not continue to live under the church's roof – otherwise, it was time to become part of the church again.

In the Church, there are always things to fix and straighten out. So you have to be able to reach those things and do something about them. If not, that means someone else is standing over them defiantly and won't let you do your job. That's not a workable situation.

- **Communication networks** – Good communications have almost always meant the difference between victory and defeat in a battle. Information has to flow freely between all levels of the organization. Orders, reports from the battlefield, needs and schedules – all this is vital information that is needed at various levels, promptly and clearly, to achieve success. The Mission is always clear to everyone, and everybody can see progress being made – which helps the spirit of the whole group tremendously.

The communication has to flow in both directions. Not only do the leaders have to communicate clearly with the members about what is going on and what the expectations and program are, the members have to communicate their needs, concerns and progress reports back to the leaders. This is so that the leadership can make necessary adjustments to the program according to the reports from the field of action, so that they are not just blindly following a plan regardless of whether it's working or not!

And one of the most fatal mistakes that anybody can make is to give in to fear of a rebuke. People will often hide or downplay a problem because they don't want to get in trouble over it. What they don't understand is that the leader's job is to fix problems, not persecute people. *They need to know about these problems.* They can't solve anything if they don't know about them. It may be that the former leader enjoyed jumping down people's throats over mistakes, but all he accomplished was to make it doubly difficult for you to find out what's going on.

> Therefore confess your sins to each other and pray for each other so that you may be healed. (James 5:16)

> Therefore, as God's chosen people, holy and dearly loved, clothe yourselves with compassion, kindness, humility, gentleness and patience. Bear with each other and forgive whatever grievances you may have against one another. Forgive as the Lord forgave you. And over all these virtues put on love, which binds them all together in perfect unity. (Colossians 3:12-14)

- **Good view of the enemy** – Remember that our enemies are unique: the world, the flesh, and the devil. The enemy is not the church down the road, or one's political enemies, or even our nasty neighbors. It's going to be an uphill fight if you have to convince the church of the reality of the devil, or that our present culture is destructive to our spiritual well-being. If the people aren't going to accept who the real enemy is, if they are too much in love with what the Christian ought to hate, you are not going to get anywhere in your ministry.

Assessment of the Position

> Still others, like seed sown among thorns, hear the word; but the worries of this life, the deceitfulness of wealth and the desires for other things come in and choke the word, making it unfruitful. (Mark 4:18-19)

One aspect of this is what people come to church to accomplish. Why are they here? If not the Mission, then what? The Mission identifies the enemy to fight. If people don't come to work on their sinful hearts, and to turn away from the world and its dark master, then they are coming for the wrong reasons, whatever they are.

- **If we are not on good ground, can we easily get there?** – Not all is lost if the church isn't on good ground. It may be that it can get there easily enough. If the church is simply ignorant about how to fight, and if they are willing to follow you to better ground, then you have real possibilities here. Examine the situation carefully to see if you can turn defeat into a victory. David found Israel in terrible shape from the mismanagement of King Saul, and in a few short years brought God's people to the height of their historical glory. But then he was an extraordinary leader.

2. How is the enemy situated?

The reason we resort to the military model is this: we are out to *destroy the enemy*. Our focus is on the enemy at all times; you have to be constantly aware of your Mission and planning for how you will deal with the enemy whenever he shows up. Let him out of your sight for a moment, or turn your attention elsewhere, and you will become his victim before you know it. It is your *job* to lead the troops to victory against the enemy.

Assessment of the Position

Therefore you have to approach any potential job with this primary function in mind.

- **Nature of enemy influence, past & present** – You must do some spiritual assessment as you study the church. Are they a spiritually healthy group, or has the enemy destroyed them so thoroughly that you basically have a lot of wounded and suffering casualties on your hands?

    One church that I know of had years of legalistic preaching from an oppressive pastor, until finally (despite their deep loyalty to leadership) even they had had enough and left. But the damage was done; the scars ran deep, and any pastor who would agree to minister to them had to address this profound legalism that would resist all news of the freshness of the Gospel of Christ.

    Another example: many modern churches are simply a religious version of the world. Their blatant materialism, their craving for entertainment, their refusal to look at their own sinful hearts, their abysmal ignorance of God and his Word – they don't know how far from the mark they really are. They are not a church, as the Bible defines a church. The pastor who takes a group like this is walking into a spiritual wasteland, and shouldn't do so with his eyes closed to the challenge before him. The enemy has been there before him doing his worst.

- **Individual and church levels** – Not all of the church will necessarily be under the influence of the enemy. The church itself may be healthy; some individual, however, may have serious spiritual issues that may or may not affect the rest of the group. Paul had to rebuke the Corinthian church for allowing a "sex offender" to remain on the church membership list.

Or it could be the other way around. You could meet someone at the church who is right on target spiritually and you get the impression that the whole church is therefore doing well, when actually this person is like Elijah among the idolatrous Israelites – one in a thousand.

- **What are the needs of the group?** – Every church will be different. Everyone is fighting a different battle against our enemies. Though we all have the same enemies, the forms of the battle – the actual battlefields where we meet them – will change considerably from group to group. You will have to discern what the particular issues are in this group and form your plans accordingly.

This is in fact what Paul was doing when he wrote his letters to the churches. The Corinthian church was dealing with simple yet serious maturity issues. The Ephesians and Colossians heard about the riches in Christ. The Philippians needed a lesson on humility, and Timothy on leadership. A good leader will be able to quickly target the needs of the group and work with them on that level.

One church that I met was a conservative island in very liberal surroundings. Massachusetts has been one of a handful of states allowing homosexual marriages, and the battle was shaping up to challenge that position in the legislature. This church stood against the issue; but you could be sure the issue would be front and center for them for months, and the battle would be hot, as they confronted their liberal neighbors with God's truth.

The battles that shake the foundations of the church are many: liberal theology, morality issues, social issues, political issues, and in many places simply the basic necessities of life as the poor and sick face disaster. Put your finger on the main issues of the group you are considering, and see if you have the resources and background to help them deal with their problems. Remember that not everyone is qualified to do this work: the disciples were completely unable to heal certain people with their limited spiritual resources; they simply could not do what Jesus could do.

- **Our weapons, skills – are they effective?** – You should take an inventory of the spiritual resources that the group has available to fight with. Do they value the Bible for what it is? Is prayer a viable option for them? Do they know anything about God? Is there a community of believers there who will stick together and follow a leader? They may not know how to use these resources, but that is easily fixed if they will follow someone who knows how to pull this situation together (hopefully you!). But if they don't have even the basic resources of what makes a church, it may not work out and you will be trying to move a dead horse in vain. There are many churches that are trying to use the world's methods to build God's Kingdom and they are failing miserably to meet people's spiritual needs.

> The weapons we fight with are not the weapons of the world. On the contrary, they have divine power to demolish strongholds. (2 Corinthians 10:4)

3. *Fatal flaws*
   - **Temptations**
   - **Sins**
   - **Heresies**
   - **Political correctness**
   - **Liberalism**
   - **Lies**

One last check. Look around for telltale signs of hidden skeletons in the closet. Not that you will see everything on this first or even second visit, but if you do some discreet snooping around and asking questions, you may discover a smoldering bomb before it goes off in your face. Like deacons sleeping around with each others' wives, or the bank closing in on a dishonest treasurer, or a professor at a liberal seminary sitting on the board of elders, or a divided and angry congregation battling over a land purchase. And you won't necessarily get this kind of information from the powers-that-be; you will more likely get it from the guy in the pew. Take someone out to lunch.

4. Are the right resources available?

We are in a spiritual battle, but we can't ignore the fact that we need physical resources to fight with. Frederick the Great said that "money is like the magician's wand" – meaning that any effort in this world requires physical resources. Jesus chided the church about being lax in this area:

> Or suppose a king is about to go to war against another king. Will he not first sit down and consider whether he is able with ten thousand men to oppose the one coming against him with twenty thousand? (Luke 14:31)

We have already looked at the importance of spiritual resources to fight the battle, but it remains to examine whether you will have the physical resources as well. Even Jesus had a few women who supported his ministry financially. You need, for example, a place to meet. You don't want to get thrown out on the street because you over-budgeted and can't pay the rent. You want the facilities to be conducive to meeting comfortably for all concerned. You need access to the facilities at the stated times as well as in times of emergency. Perhaps you can split the group into several homes for certain types of functions.

Assessment of the Position

I know of a church (probably many more are like this) that saddled itself with a multi-million dollar educational building for the children. The problem was that a national credit disaster suddenly threatened the church with foreclosure, since the members were finding it difficult to pay for this white elephant. Their grand dreams were not only putting their educational plans at risk, but the whole church as well. In desperation to keep the building afloat, they made plans to reorganize their program and start basketball teams, book clubs – anything to attract more youth to the building, which actually only served to steer the church *away* from its true Mission. We are not supposed to identify the Church with games and fun; we have to organize around the right things, and then people will know where to come when they need those things.

Believe it or not, it is not necessary to build grand physical buildings to make a viable church. The church is not the building; it's the people in the building. You should have enough facility to enable the work of the church, but you don't want that physical side to drag down the work of the spiritual. It's not fair to the church to invest in huge building programs and then insist they pay for it. Their only financial obligation, according to the Bible, is to support the teaching ministry and take care of the poor.

> The elders who direct the affairs of the church well are worthy of double honor, especially those whose work is preaching and teaching. For the Scripture says, "Do not muzzle the ox while it is treading out the grain," and "The worker deserves his wages." (1 Timothy 5:17-18)

> Religion that God our Father accepts as pure and faultless is this: to look after orphans and widows in their distress and to keep oneself from being polluted by the world. (James 1:27)

Anything else is a decision that has to be made by the entire group and should be strictly in line with what will

Assessment of the Position

accomplish the Mission, no more – and certainly not put it at risk.

5. Is there one commander at the top?

Even though modern Americans really hate to "give control" to one person in the church, there's no question that one leader at the top is the best model for church organization. All the problems that people are worried about can easily be addressed with the right balance-of-powers system. The problems arising from a lack of a single leader will, however, eventually destroy the church's ability to achieve the Mission. A democratic system in a church only looks peaceful on the outside; actually they aren't accomplishing anything meaningful. A multiplicity of wills has the Mission deadlocked, with the result that the church is tied up with bazaars and community suppers and with kindergarten-level sermons that offend only the intelligent.

I think the main reason that people in churches don't like a single leader at the top is because they don't want to be told what to do. They want the freedom to do whatever they like, when they like. But that's not the way Jesus told us to operate in the church. It's a hierarchy: Christ is at the top, his Apostles below him, the under-shepherds below them, and then the rest of the church. It's a top-down approach to management. Only a strong leadership can successfully tackle the goals of the church. If a church member doesn't like this model, then he/she is actually in rebellion against the King who set it all up this way.

> If the world hates you, keep in mind that it hated me first. If you belonged to the world, it would love you as its own. As it is, you do not belong to the world, but I have chosen you out of the world. That is why the world hates you. Remember the words I spoke to you: 'No servant

Assessment of the Position

> is greater than his master.' If they persecuted me, they will persecute you also. If they obeyed my teaching, they will obey yours also. They will treat you this way because of my Name, for they do not know the One who sent me. (John 15:18-21)

Therefore, you want to be especially alert to how willing they are to follow Christ's will. Since your job will be to communicate his will to the church, that's the same thing as asking how willing they are to follow *you*.

- **Are the elders supportive of my leading?** – Let's use the word "elder" for the ruling members of a church group, though not all churches use that Biblical word. It simply refers to the decision-makers, the leaders who lead and teach the group. They may be official or unofficial, since in some churches they pride themselves on having no titles (though the fact is that there *are* leaders in every church group!).

  What you are looking for is a willingness on the elders' part to let you lead them. I don't think most churches appreciate the fact that a new pastor, trained and ready to implement Biblical principles, is far more qualified to do this job than most church elders are. Elders are usually taken from secular employment and given spiritual responsibilities for which they were poorly, if ever, trained. They know almost nothing about theology, ecclesiology, church history, hermeneutics, even counseling. They know embarrassingly little about the Bible itself. If you have your hands tied by self-proclaimed experts who won't let you do your job, because they think they know better what is needed than you do, you will get nowhere. It does seem strange to me that churches insist on a seminary-trained pastor, yet they try to tell him how to do his job!

  > Don't let anyone look down on you because you are young, but set an example for the

> believers in speech, in life, in love, in faith and in purity. (1 Timothy 4:12)

You can't have two leaders at the top. If the elders want you to be part of an elder team, fine – but somehow you have to be the "head elder" if this thing is going to work. Two or more equal elders with no one person to make the final decision is a recipe for disaster. Napoleon once said that he would much rather fight against two good generals than one bad general – the point being that a battle of wills is going to ruin things when the time comes to make a critical decision. Business understands this, government understands this, the military understands this, even families understand this – it's time for the church to catch up now.

Usually what everyone is concerned about is curbing your passions and correcting you if you go wrong. There's nothing wrong with that; it's Biblical to submit your judgment and actions to the other "prophets" who can correct you if necessary.

> The spirits of prophets are subject to the control of prophets. (1 Corinthians 14:32)

The problems that come up concerning a pastor's leadership are not serious enough to scrap the system. Even outright failure can be fixed with Biblical procedures. But to do away with strong leadership is fatal to the life of the church and can't be fixed; giving away decisive and clear leadership is to accept chaos.

Form a clear process, a Biblical protocol, for bringing accountability to your job. If you don't do your job well, they can always find someone else. But it would be fatal to be forced to give in, over and over, to people who don't know what they are doing when it's obvious to everyone else that you do. The well-being of the congregation depends on your expertise, and it will

Assessment of the Position

often depend on you being able to make decisions (with the help of the other elders) and executing them without being stymied by the bad judgment of the rest of the team, untrained as they are. They just have to trust you here.

- **How qualified are the leaders?** – Another aspect of the elders' condition is how qualified they are to continue as leaders in the church. No doubt they have spent years leading the church in their own way; but that way may have been unprofitable and even downright destructive of spiritual growth. If so, you are going to have to replace them with more qualified leaders. If that's impossible, you are probably walking into a problem situation that you won't be able to solve – especially if the church really likes them. The Bible lays great stress on the qualifications of the elders.

> Now the overseer must be above reproach, the husband of but one wife, temperate, self-controlled, respectable, hospitable, able to teach, not given to drunkenness, not violent but gentle, not quarrelsome, not a lover of money. He must manage his own family well and see that his children obey him with proper respect. (1 Timothy 3:2-4)

The ideal would be if you can easily show them their need for further training, and if they become willing to follow you.

- **What are they in charge of now?** – You want to find out what the elders are in charge of. Usually they aren't in charge of anything; they like to rule, but they don't like to teach or do other functions in the church. But if they are in charge of various aspects of the church's ministry you will want to see if they are capable, whether they are trained for the job, whether they are making progress, what others think of their leadership, whether they are facing problems that they will need

Assessment of the Position

your help to solve, and so on. Find out how much of the church structure depends on the existing leadership, and then decide whether it needs massive changes or can be used as is.

- **Are there isolated commands?** – Often you will find that a particular job was given to a leader years ago, and now there's no moving him or her out of that position. You have no doubt seen or heard of this in music programs: a very capable young woman inherited the choir and piano, and now fifty years later she's still at her post, a distraction to the whole congregation because she can't play well anymore. And nobody has the courage to replace her! What you don't want is a situation where someone is sitting on their job, like a hen on her egg, when they don't belong there – especially if they never did belong there. If that problem isn't solvable, you may want to consider that situation and let it figure into your decision. It depends on how big an issue it could become.

- **Are there overlapping commands?** – One strange thing that happens in some churches is that two different leaders control the same functions in the church, or their areas of responsibility overlap. This often leads to war in the church. The least that will happen is that people will be confused as to who is the leader and whose orders they are to follow, and parties will form up dividing the church.

There must not be overlapping commands. If you don't have a clear division of labor in the church, either make that plain in the beginning that this problem has to be solved, or seriously consider turning down the job. You particularly don't want someone taking over parts of your job!

Remember Napoleon's comment about fighting against two good generals rather than one bad general? The enemy knows how to take advantage of the chaos and inter-fighting that will likely happen when two or more people are in charge of the same thing. Wills clash, nobody is willing to back down, and the program comes to a halt. So, make a clear hierarchy for the responsibilities of a church; bad or incompetent leaders can always be replaced. But when everyone is in charge, nobody can be replaced.

- **Any alliances present?** – People form cliques in most churches. They tend to gravitate to other people of like mind and persuasion. You want to find out where those close groups are, if you can, before taking on the job.

An individual can only do so much in the church; but a group of individuals can do so much more. There's a certain loyalty in the group, they see things in the same light, they are after the same things. There's nothing wrong with having friends and hanging out together, but there's everything wrong with having a stronger loyalty to your particular group at the expense of the church – and especially the leadership. Cliques can split a church. In one church, the membership split along the lines of age: the older ones fiercely defended the traditions of the church, and the younger group identified with the growing Charismatic movement of the seventies and pushed for radical change in the church. Neither group was pushing for the Mission, just for issues that served their own purposes. It made for continual warfare.

In another church, there was a group of women in charge of the youth program who defiantly rejected elder after elder who tried and failed to bring them into the overall church program. Obviously they didn't have Christ's Kingdom at heart; not only were they unwilling to learn, they had no respect for authority over them. In becoming their own authority, they rejected Christ's authority.

Assessment of the Position

- **What would it take to fire me?** – What I mean by this is, can the church fire you simply because you irritated them with some soul-searching in your sermons? Can someone's whim – someone who has an inordinate influence with the rest of the church – remove you from office because they don't like you?

The ideal is that you can only be removed from your job because you weren't doing your job – as Christ defined it. If the Lord Jesus himself would find fault with you for being an unfaithful shepherd of his flock, then there would be reason enough to remove you. And to determine that will require some discerning elders who know how to pray and study the Word. That's the kind of job you want. But if it's all too easy to fire you over the caprice of dissatisfied "customers," you are asking for trouble taking that job.

There's a serious misconception in today's churches: that the pastor is an employee of the church. It came about, naturally enough, when the job was turned into a career with specialized educational training, and the churches started attaching a paycheck to the job with schedules and duties, and elders and church members formed "search committees" who sat in judgment of prospective candidates. After this Americanization of the position, it makes sense why churches consider their pastors to be employees. But this hamstrings the pastor so that he can't do his job the way he needs to do it. That's like calling a shepherd the employee of the sheep that he's responsible for.

His employer is actually Christ, not the church; his "paycheck" is the church's way of making sure he doesn't have to worry about paying his bills (not as their rewarding him for his labors); his duties are outlined already in the Bible. He must present the Word of God in the way God told him to present it, fear no man because of it, and answer to the King for his performance. I'm not sure what it will take to change the American church back into the Biblical model, but this idea of an "employee" has to change if we hope to get anywhere with the Mission.

6. Can I achieve the objective?

The bottom line is this: given all the factors, are enough of the necessary elements in place for this job to be workable? Can you reasonably expect to achieve your Mission with this group? Certainly no position will be perfect; God usually will take up the slack and make it work. But you have to discern if even God has given up on this group; the signs should be there.

> She named the boy Ichabod, saying, "The glory has departed from Israel" — because of the capture of the ark of God and the deaths of her father-in-law and her husband. She said, "The glory has departed from Israel, for the ark of God has been captured." (1 Samuel 4:21-22)

> Remember the height from which you have fallen! Repent and do the things you did at first. If you do not repent, I will come to you and remove your lampstand from its place. (Revelation 2:5)

No doubt, over the last 2000 years, the Lord Jesus has removed his lampstand from many a church. You don't want to walk into a situation like that. Use some discernment; don't underestimate serious problems. Be willing to walk away from a losing situation.

- **Is it open to tactics, methods?** – Can you reasonably expect that you can use the procedures and methodology that the Bible taught you and get somewhere? Or are there circumstances and elements in this group that make that impossible?

Assessment of the Position

- **Is everyone willing?** – Can you discern a willingness on the people's part – and the other leaders – to grow spiritually, to change, to conform themselves to the Lord's will more and more? Or can you detect a solid resistance to change, an arrogance in the position they already hold?

- **Does everything look feasible?** – Generally speaking, do you think you can work with these people? Is there anything that stands out like a red flag, alerting you to something that would bring everything to a halt down the road? Or does it feel like a good fit after all of your research?

- **Will it take a short or long-range strategy?** – It may be feasible, but how long will it take? Are there burdens here that the group is still working with from the past that have to be dealt with first before you can get down to your primary task? Church splits, for example, often leave raw edges that take many years to heal; people often can't hear what you say because of the trauma that they have just come out of. They don't trust pastors anymore, for good or bad reasons. Maybe this job is for you, but you may have to adjust your expectations of a quick turnaround.

- **How much drill and training are required?** – Are you going to have to start from ground zero with these people? Will you have to de-program them first from heresies or bad practices? Or are they students at heart? Will they willingly show up for spiritual training? Or are they the laid-back type, used to letting the pastor do all the work?

- **Which pillars are present, which missing?** – Go back and review the five pillars of the church, the five functions that help us achieve our Mission. Which ones are missing? Which ones are weak? Where is the church strong? Your first task will be to rebuild here, to make sure the church is founded on the Mission and

Assessment of the Position

able to proceed towards its objective. If not, *can* it be done?

Summary

This has been an extensive analysis of the kind of reconnaissance that you need to do before accepting a church position, but hopefully I have made you aware of how important it is to get a full picture. I don't want you to think that, if you see some problems along the way, it's an automatic reason to reject the job. No church is perfect; that's why you are being sent there – to work on their problems! It's just that there *are* some problems that are best left to some other person who has special skills to solve them. If you decide, therefore, that this job isn't for you, you may want to make your reasons known to the church itself, out of Christian charity, so that they know you rejected their offer for reasons that will cause them to take a more skilled person's offer seriously.

It's not a bad idea to keep coming back to this kind of analysis even after you have accepted a position. As the leader, it's your responsibility to keep your finger on the pulse of the situation at all times. And these areas are the first level of information sources about a church. If there are any changes about a group's spiritual health, they will eventually (like a germ making its presence known through a fever) become apparent on the public level. It's wisdom to keep track of that so that you are not the last person to find out.

ASSUMING COMMAND

The leader has to provide the direction, the energy, and the vision of the Mission if he wants the troops to follow him. He also has to keep his finger on the pulse of the army, in all of its details. He must organize the troops skillfully to be an effective fighting unit.

ASSUMING COMMAND

If you take the job, you have your work cut out for you. The key here is to not make any wrong assumptions. Supposing that you are trained and ready to handle this position of church leadership, *you* will have to set the pace for everyone else. You will be making decisions for organization, training, discipline, supply, fighting the enemy, and getting everyone to the objective. And you can't assume that everyone will understand what you are doing, let alone be willing to help you.

There are certain things that you will have to do to clear the ground for action, so to speak. There are obstacles to clear away if you want to make progress.

The Starting Point

There are some assumptions that you *have* to make; this will get you started off on the right foot. You have to plan for every contingency and lay the right foundation if you want things to work in the future.

- **Form new teams, re-train** – No doubt your predecessor had his own team to work with, and it's probably still in place when you move in. Over the years certain people have assumed positions or functions in the church that they expect to remain in control of. You will also encounter great resistance if you try to change those arrangements.

    The goal here is not to keep people happy, but to get the right people in place. A new President routinely replaces the cabinet of the former President to make room for his own team. You need people who are in step with your methods and goals; you are going to make a lot of vital changes in the church, and at this point you don't need people who are going to stand in your way.

One pastor that I know of took a job at a church and sat through a couple of painful Sunday School sessions led by a woman who was in no way qualified to teach that class. He decided that this situation had to change immediately if the class was to learn anything about the Bible. He offered to give her a "break" – she was actually looking for a little time off anyway – and he assumed the class for her. Needless to say, he didn't offer her the job back; and when someone came in who was qualified to teach it, he turned it over to the new person instead. Lesson: *you can't cater to someone's feelings when the spiritual health of the group is at stake*. You *can* find gentle ways to make changes, but don't hesitate to make those changes.

One more point: you may as well assume that very few people will understand what you are after. Very few Christians understand the Mission clearly, let alone how to accomplish it. People who thought they knew the Bible are going to surprise you with how much they don't know. Even elders often don't know enough about the Bible to teach it. The average church member's grasp of the truth is about on the level of primary school; they haven't devoted time or energy to focus on a mastery of the Bible. It's time to dig out the lessons on the fundamentals of the faith and start there. Rebuild on that foundation, and save the deeper material till later, when you are convinced that they can handle it. You certainly don't want to make false assumptions and then find out the hard way, during battle, that your trusted helper easily falls prey to a heresy or cult.

- **Make the Mission clear** – Every church has a "mission statement," but I've seen so many of them that had nothing to do with Biblical principles that I feel we have to start from the beginning here also.

It's amazing to me how many churches, even Christians of spiritual stature, seem to miss the objectives of our faith. John Wesley, for example, who was a shining light in the history of the church, seemed to miss part of the picture. He published his **Forty-four Sermons** as a representative collection of all the sermons he preached over his many years of service. He absolutely nailed the first part of the Mission – to be saved from our sins. Few church leaders were so ruthless in his attack on that enemy; I wish the modern church were so ruthless. But he made almost no mention of the second part of the Mission: to get ready to live with God in Heaven forever. You will look in vain for that emphasis. As if our Christian life was for this world only! There is a tremendous amount of work that must be done in this area, and if we ignore it we will suffer greatly as a result.

It is critical that the entire group knows where it is going. You must make it clear from the beginning what you, and they, will be working on. This serves two purposes: first, you will all be working on the same thing; and second, you can design every function around that Mission and everyone will understand why. If someone doesn't want to work on that Mission, that's another matter; they can go to a church of their choice. But here, "we will serve the LORD."

- **Start with the basics** – It deserves repeating that the average church member knows very little about the Bible. You may as well get ready for that disappointment. Every Tom, Dick and Harry think they know more than the pastor, but you can easily back these so-called "experts" to the wall with a challenge to support their ignorant statements from the Bible. They can't.

In our present culture there are literally millions who don't know who Jesus was. The majority of church-goers don't believe in the devil, or Hell. It goes without saying that the Biblical account of Creation, or the Flood, or of any miracles for that matter, are considered myths, and the scientists know best what happened in the past. Most church members can't find the Old Testament Prophets. And these are just the issues that deal with Biblical literacy. When it comes to the great themes of the Bible, you will probably find an appalling ignorance of them.

Not that our generation is particularly worse than others in history; mankind in general has been apathetic about spiritual matters. Just don't make the mistake of trusting that church members necessarily know what they are talking about. You can safely assume the opposite. "An army is composed for the most part of idle and inactive men," Frederick the Great stated from experience. They need the leader to push them into training. So get ready to teach spiritual children.

> We have much to say about this, but it is hard to explain because you are slow to learn. In fact, though by this time you ought to be teachers, you need someone to teach you the elementary truths of God's Word all over again. You need milk, not solid food! (Hebrews 5:11-12)

- **There will be resistance** – People don't like change, for many reasons. Either they are comfortable, or they feel that they are already good enough, or they don't like to be led. And some will have more sinister reasons: they don't like the Mission. They want to continue in their sins, and they have no interest in God. And this is in the Church!

  > You snakes! You brood of vipers! How will you escape being condemned to hell? Therefore I am sending you prophets and wise men and

> teachers. Some of them you will kill and crucify; others you will flog in your synagogues and pursue from town to town. And so upon you will come all the righteous blood that has been shed on earth, from the blood of righteous Abel to the blood of Zechariah son of Berekiah, whom you murdered between the temple and the altar. (Matthew 23:33-35)

Steel yourself against this inevitable reaction, but do the right thing. The typical American, for the sake of peace, will do just about anything to get others to think well of him; we don't like conflict, especially in the church among church leaders. Of all places, why must there be war in the sphere of love? So many times I have seen the pastor encounter bitter resistance, even open war, against his leadership and it throws him completely into emotional turmoil and paralysis. He didn't think he would run into so much resistance when he was only trying to help people. Eventually many burn out and quit the ministry completely.

It's not necessary for people to like you; it's necessary for you to do your job and train these people in survival skills. It's for their good; but like little children, they are going to complain and grumble and cause trouble all the way to the Promised Land! You *are* responsible to the Shepherd, however, to feed and lead these ignorant sheep to their home. If you get discouraged from the trouble they give you and give up, their blood will be on your head. Leaders have to have thick skin; it's just part of the job. There have hardly been any leaders in history who didn't encounter resistance from their followers.

Form a Team

You are going to need a team to work with you. There is so much to do in a church, and you simply don't have the spiritual gifts to do it all, let alone the time and energy for it. But you will find that the Lord of the Church is not negligent about his own house; he will provide all the necessary resources to achieve the Mission successfully.

- **Find the willing** – Since what you have to do will be so new to everyone, you are going to have to find helpers who are willing to follow. That will be no small task. The first item on their agenda is extensive training! They will need to know the Bible to a greater and deeper degree than the average member. They need to discipline their lives to focus on the Mission. They need a love for the flock, so that they will stretch their lives and their resources to do whatever necessary to help others achieve their spiritual objectives. Not everyone in the church will be like this; but you can't do your job without a team of willing elders (call them what you will, the Bible describes their functions) behind you and helping you at every step.

  Your troops will be willing on your day of battle.
  (Psalm 110:3)

- **Isolate the unwilling** – The other side of that coin is to discourage those who want to be leaders but, for some reason, could never do the job. Somehow you are going to have to keep ignorant, self-willed and immoral people out of positions of leadership. Volunteers are nice, but not if they are not willing to train and take on the necessary responsibilities. Don't sacrifice the spiritual well-being of the group just to bring someone on board (or keep them in a position they already have) who has no intention of changing *their* ways.

- **Form a method of dealing with problems** – "In this world you will have trouble." Expect problems; plan for them. You would do well to plan for dealing with different kinds of problems, and various troublemakers, way ahead of time. Don't be surprised by unexpected behavior that you "didn't think would happen in our group." Anything can, and does, happen in a church. Come up with procedures, protocols, disciplinary methods – and then follow them faithfully when those issues come up. If you have procedures in place for these kinds of things, the church will feel confident in your ability to handle problems of any sort. It's the uncertainty, confusion, and bewilderment that happens in the face of trouble that often throws a whole church out of balance, and then is when opportunists have the chance to take control away from you.

- **Implement accelerated training program** – Leaders need skills that the average church member either doesn't need, or will grow into more slowly. Your first task is to bring them up to speed quickly so that they can get started doing their jobs. Leaders have to teach the Bible; therefore they require a sufficient grasp of the Bible to teach it well. That means their training in the Bible has to be intense, focused, continuous, and open to testing. Leaders need to pray; therefore they need training in the great issues of the Kingdom and how to bring them to the throne of grace. Leaders have to be moral examples in the flock; therefore they have to put everything in their lives under the microscope of God's Word and change now, before they bring the work of the church into disrepute in the community.

> An elder must be blameless, the husband of but one wife, a man whose children believe and are not open to the charge of being wild and disobedient. Since an overseer is entrusted with God's work, he must be blameless – not overbearing, not quick-tempered, not given to drunkenness, not violent, not pursuing dishonest gain. (Titus 1:6-7)

This is one reason that Paul counseled the church to refrain from putting the spiritually young in positions of authority in the church. They simply have not had time to get this organized, spiritually speaking. They also haven't seen the need yet for such introspection and correction; it's not without reason that wisdom and age often go together. Everyone knows that you can't tell a young person anything they don't already know; but an older, wiser person never stops learning.

> He must not be a recent convert, or he may become conceited and fall under the same judgment as the devil. (1 Timothy 3:6)

- **Have division of labor** – Your team is made up of different kinds of people with different skills. You must learn how to distribute responsibilities among the team. For one thing, you are not called on to do the whole job! Jesus doesn't want you to. He expects others to carry their part of the load, and he has given them the necessary abilities to do that. If you try to do it all, you will burn out quickly.

> There are different kinds of gifts, but the same Spirit. There are different kinds of service, but the same Lord. There are different kinds of working, but the same God works all of them in all men. (1 Corinthians 12:4-6)

Second, you will grow to appreciate those leaders who can do things that you can't do: counsel various people in the church when you wouldn't know what to say, or motivate church members to holy living while you are in the study getting ready for a sermon.

The point is to be big enough to allow for other workers. Instead of being a threat to you, or invading your special territory, you must see them as necessary allies in your endeavor. If you are doing your job well, the church members won't think less of your importance to the Mission just because others are doing their job well too. The butcher, the baker, and the candlestick-maker all come together to form a viable community.

Plus, there's protection in numbers. Troublemakers in the church have a field day when there's a single person to blame for problems. Pastors usually have a big red target on their chest anyway (the wicked see it plainly!), and the work of a church will often come to a standstill when people of evil intentions are shooting relentlessly at the poor man. It's much harder for people to make trouble when there are two, three, or four elders doing the work; then it becomes plainer that the real problem is the troublemaker himself, not the leaders.

As far as specific tasks, divide them up according to the skills of the leadership team and of the church as a whole.

- **Lieutenants** – You will need "right-hand men" to help you think through situations, make decisions, and carry out tasks in the church. You aren't looking for "yes-men" but capable helpers who share your vision and your desire to see the Kingdom grow in Christ's way. Paul had his Epaphroditus and Titus and Timothy.

- **Engineers** – In the military, these people are responsible for building fortifications, bridges, roads, encampments, and whatever else is necessary for the army to carry out its tasks, either defensive or offensive. We will look at what engineering requirements are necessary in the church later.

- **Logistics, supply depots** – Logistics is the science of getting the necessary supplies to the troops when they need them, and transporting troops to the battlefield. In the church, this is where the teachers come in.

- **Outposts** – When the army is encamped, someone has to keep a watch out for the enemy. They have to stand guard when the army is asleep. They have to prevent surprise by the enemy, and if possible try to find out what the enemy is doing. There is plenty of opportunity for this in the church, and great need of it.

- **Reconnaissance team** – The leadership needs information and lots of it in order to make informed decisions. We will look at the duties of reconnaissance later and what kinds of information that the leaders need.

All these form a well-organized team that can meet any contingency.

- **Communication** – Your team can't operate well unless there is complete communication among all members. Everyone has to know what's going on. And you need to set up the procedures and situations that will make this communication happen: regular meetings, reports, emails, phone calls, conferences, newsletters, etc.

Free communication means that there will be no surprises among members, or hidden agendas. Everyone will understand the Mission and what action is being taken by the group. It will promote group-think – the ability to put more than one head on a problem and solve it quickly and efficiently. If everyone understands that they can get your ear, and that you will take them seriously, they will be more willing to let you lead and make the final decisions.

Keep in mind, too, that people will be afraid to tell you anything if you are the type to blow up at them in anger or frustration. You will always have problems, but don't take it out on your elders or teachers if you value their openness. Encourage dialog, questions, discussions – just don't let things degenerate into fights.

Paul, for example, was perfectly willing to teach those who would listen, but he didn't have time for a fight; there were more important matters to work on.

> All of us who are mature should take such a view of things. And if on some point you think differently, that too God will make clear to you. Only let us live up to what we have already attained. (Philippians 3:15-16)

The Marines have a policy about communication: commanders don't chew off the heads of their subordinates if they make a mistake. They can learn from mistakes. The leaders are trying to encourage initiative even at the lower levels; they would rather the lieutenant make a mistake trying to do his job than do nothing at all. That spirit keeps trust between the levels, and communication open and free.

There's something else about the Marines that amuses the average civilian: he YELLS his responses back to the drill sergeants. But they are not playing games. The greatest need in communication is to be loud and clear. A mumbled, garbled, unintelligible answer is useless to those in command. They need to know right away whether their order was heard and understood; if not, they will have to try again. Events in a battle are often fast and furious, and there's a lot of noise going on that can make things confusing. So they need those answers fired right back at them.

Declare the Mission

Things done in secret are suspect and misunderstood. If you aren't up front with what you are doing, people will think you are up to no good. So the best thing to do is make the Mission statement plain from the very beginning.

This Mission is, after all, the core of the message of the Bible. If anybody is offended with it, it's because they have serious moral problems. That's what Paul meant about the offense of the Gospel:

> For the message of the cross is foolishness to those who are perishing, but to us who are being saved it is the power of God. (1 Corinthians 1:18)

> For we are to God the aroma of Christ among those who are being saved and those who are perishing. To the one we are the smell of death; to the other, the fragrance of life. (2 Corinthians 2:15-16)

The point of Christianity is to save us from our sins, and to give us a perfect righteousness (Christ's) so that we might live with God. When this is clearly understood, it keeps the church focused: we know what we are supposed to do, and we will always be wary about what others might want us to do that has nothing to do with the Mission.

People like grand beginnings, because it seems to give an air of authority and common acceptability to the project. When everyone is behind it and excited about it, they feel there's a good chance of succeeding. Solomon inaugurated the new Temple by gathering all of Israel to Jerusalem to celebrate its opening. It was an event that captured everyone's imagination; they remembered it all their lives and passed down the story to succeeding generations. It identified Israel's purpose, and gave a direction to the whole country. It pulled all of Israel around the cause.

So, you need to kick off the beginning of your ministry in the same way. The goal is not the show itself, but fixing the purpose of the church firmly in people's minds and memory. So wave the flag. They need a cause to fight for, and this is the right cause. Give it to them plainly, on center stage, right up front. This Mission will be new to them anyway, so you may as well make it look new.

Of course you will be expecting everyone to sign on at that point. It's going to be hard for an individual to resist the Lord's program when the whole group is gathering around to support it. Later, when someone causes trouble, it will be an easy matter to remind them what they signed up for.

And you have to make plain to them that the training, the functions, the progress of the church will be around this Mission statement. They should know that the church's focus will be this from now on. They are signing up to work; they are agreeing to throw themselves into reaching this goal. You may or may not let them know at this point how much work it will be, but they must understand that there's a task in front of them and it will take all of their dedication and energy to pull it off. Everyone is a soldier in Christ's army, and everyone will have a job to do. The responsibility is everyone's, and the rewards will belong to everyone.

Make it plain, also, about the five pillars of the church – the God-given principles that make the Mission happen. We are not just going to charge down the road with no plan and expect to reach our goal! Later you will have time to expand on these principles, build them into your organization, and run the church according to them. For now, however, everyone needs to understand that the Lord has given them the *means* of accomplishing the Mission. It's a wise move to let them know this up front, so that they won't start throwing their own ideas at you later on and expecting you to take them seriously.

With a clear Mission statement, and a solid plan for getting there, you will have what you need to gather the troops behind you and get started.

Create a schedule

Planning extends to scheduling. It's essential that certain things have to happen and in the right order. Nobody else is going to think of doing this; it's your responsibility to create a time-table.

You have to prioritize events. You have to make sure certain things happen, in the right order. You have to time events as much as possible. Of course circumstances will change over time, and your schedule will start getting out of focus and more difficult to stick to.

When this happens, just re-schedule along the way to reflect the changing requirements.

- **Organization** – Since everyone will have a job to do, and you don't want overlapping responsibilities in the group, it's up to you to assign tasks and the places in the hierarchy. You can start with the highest levels – the elders and deacons – and as time unfolds, and as you discover who does what best and where they belong, you can fit them into their proper places in the organizational chart. The goal here is to cover all the necessary tasks.

- **Training covered** – Everyone will need training for their jobs. Remember that you can't count on anybody really understanding the Mission at the beginning, let alone their role in achieving it. You will have your hands full in this area.

  Fortunately you don't have to do it all at once. You have to start training your own team first; then as they get the skills to help you, you can assign them the tasks of training others in the church. Not every job will be required at first, so you can postpone some training until later, closer to the events that will require it. And the need for training at different levels – beginners, intermediate, advanced – in whatever area of the church will require some advanced scheduling to make sure the training process doesn't slow down, and the needs of the church are satisfactorily met along the way.

- **Formation of ministries** – You will have to lay out the essential functions of the church ahead of time and plan for getting each department trained and running efficiently. Your elder team comes first; they are the ones who will help you tremendously with the rest of the program. Follow the guidance of the Bible concerning the functions that are essential in the Church: Acts and Paul's letters will help you a great deal here. Impress on the members that these gifts will require a great deal of focused training and drills, and schedule those drill sessions to make sure they happen.

One other thing – the military understands that one training session does not a soldier make! The soldier is *always* training. People little understand the stress, the confusion, the highly-charged emotions that can overwhelm us in times of battle. It takes a great deal of studying, training and practicing to instill the kind of discipline needed under fire. Don't listen to people complaining about how much drill they have to endure! The training must be continuous; it's up to you to be creative and motivational to keep people at it.

- **Battles** – It may seem strange to schedule battles, but it will help your church members tremendously if they can use this training once in a while in a scheduled, live event. Your evangelism team, for instance: don't keep them in the classroom all the time. Send them out in controlled circumstances, with you overseeing them, and let them get a taste of battle. If you drilled them properly ahead of time, they will come back excited like Jesus' disciples, ready for more:

    > The seventy-two returned with joy and said, "Lord, even the demons submit to us in your name." (Luke 10:17)

    Their complaints over drills will turn into zeal to learn more, when they see the purpose for all this training.

    A postscript: don't forget to "de-brief" them after the event. Make them think through what they just did, why the training helped, and what could be done to make it better.

- **Movement – depots – supply lines – fortresses** – An army on the move is going to need many things along the way. War is not simply the process of carrying your gun out to look for someone to shoot. Someone has to do a lot of planning beforehand to make sure the troops have the necessary supplies, to get those supplies distributed along the route to the battlefield, to care for the wounded, to set up communications, to provide security on the flanks, to provide a safe refuge in case of retreat – on and on the list goes. There are many long months invested at headquarters behind all this planning. If you would make a list of how much work goes into all this planning, you will probably find that the actual battle takes up much less than 1% of an army's time and efforts! We will get into these specifics in more detail later on. In the meantime, lay out your schedule in preparation to work on them.

Reconnaissance

An army commander needs information like a soldier needs bullets. He can't do his job without it. If he's in the dark about anything, the battle could very well be lost.

You have to set up means of getting that information. You will be able to get some of it yourself, but you may as well plan on enlisting the help of others. You need eyes and ears everywhere in the camp, as well as out there on the battlefield watching the enemy. If you are surprised by something you didn't see coming at you, you will be held accountable for the disaster; it's your job to find out these things ahead of time and be ready for anything.

- **Demographics** – Do some research on what the group is made up of: rich or poor, locals or long-distance, young or old, sick or healthy, educated or not, well-versed in the Bible or ignorant, willing or unwilling, families or singles – everything you can learn about them. Not only do you need to know this for meeting their needs, but you will also be using this information for assignment of tasks.

Assuming Command

> Brothers, think of what you were when you were called. Not many of you were wise by human standards; not many were influential; not many were of noble birth. (1 Corinthians 1:26)

> To the Jews I became like a Jew, to win the Jews. To those under the law I became like one under the law (though I myself am not under the law), so as to win those under the law. To those not having the law I became like one not having the law (though I am not free from God's law but am under Christ's law), so as to win those not having the law. To the weak I became weak, to win the weak. I have become all things to all men so that by all possible means I might save some. (1 Corinthians 9:20-22)

You have to know the weak points in the group as well as the strong points. A large high-school group, for instance, may bring in the debilitating trends of their peers in school, and thus will be a liability in the church that has to be addressed.

- ***Esprit* of the group** – "*Esprit*" is the military term for the spirit of the group. Are they "gung-ho" about the cause? How aware are they of being a team? Are they willing to jump in and get the job done? Do they know what's at stake, and are they willing to do whatever it takes to reach the objective? Or is there something that is depressing them, discouraging them, or taking their minds and hearts away from the objective?

> I know your deeds, that you are neither cold nor hot. I wish you were either one or the other! So, because you are lukewarm — neither hot nor cold — I am about to spit you out of my mouth. (Revelation 3:15-16)

We will discuss more about developing and maintaining the *esprit* of the group in a later chapter.

- **Issues being dealt with** – Almost every group has something they are dealing with: their peculiar history, the community they are in, problematic people, theological problems, financial crises, disorganization, lack of communication, and so on. You have to find out what's on their hearts and take their issues seriously if you want them on your side. Paul kept tabs on what was going on in the Corinthian church, and addressed its serious problems so that they could get them out of the way and get back to work on the Kingdom.

- **Physical plant** – Make a complete inventory of the physical assets of the group: the place they are meeting in, the supplies and furniture and sound system, the bills outstanding, their savings, vehicles, etc. Not only do you need to know what's available for training and service, but you will have to figure out what you may still need to get to enable your plans.

- **Identify needs** – Try to discern what the spiritual needs of the group are. If they need to go back to the basics, then your training has to start there, as much as you would love to accelerate them into deeper issues. The author of Hebrews, for example, wanted to take his readers into the deep mysteries of Melchizedek, but he realized they weren't ready for that; they needed to go back over the basics again.

If there are sins that they are grappling with, you have to identify them and remove them from the field before you start plowing. If many members are struggling with the necessities of life – or, on the other side of that coin, riches are clouding some people's spiritual judgment – then you will have to direct your energies toward solving those problems.

> But the one who is rich should take pride in his low position, because he will pass away like a wild flower. For the sun rises with scorching heat and withers the plant; its blossom falls and

> its beauty is destroyed. In the same way, the rich man will fade away even while he goes about his business. (James 1:10-11)

Problems are like stumbling stones. The Spirit of God is good at removing the "things that make men stumble", so focus their attention on the work of the Spirit and coming more and more under his guiding influence.

> Therefore, since we are surrounded by such a great cloud of witnesses, let us throw off everything that hinders and the sin that so easily entangles, and let us run with perseverance the race marked out for us. (Hebrews 12:1)

- **Power centers** – Find out who are the unofficial leaders of the group. Some of these people are going to be leaders whether you like it or not. Either you will have to get those people on your side (so that the rest will follow) or you will have to single them out and separate them from the rest, so that they aren't such a counter-influence to what you are trying to do.

- **Individual talents** – This is an all-important task for you. It will be up to you to identify those in the group who have talents and abilities who can assist you and help the group grow spiritually.

> I commend to you our sister Phoebe, a servant of the church in Cenchrea. I ask you to receive her in the Lord in a way worthy of the saints and to give her any help she may need from you, for she has been a great help to many people, including me. (Romans 16:1-2)

Assume (because it's true!) that the Lord has put those gifts in the group, and do your best to find them as soon as you can, so that you can get those people busy as soon as possible.

- **Individual liabilities** – Sometimes you would love to get someone started in training, but they have their own personal issues to clear out of the way first. "Lord, first let me go and bury my father." Don't ignore those liabilities; take them seriously. It's a real mistake to put someone in as a teacher, for example, only to find out that they are facing bankruptcy or going to the divorce court. For certain jobs in the church, most people are already aware that you may need to do background checks – you don't want a convicted child-molester in the nursery!

- **System flow; how things get done** – Make friends with the office workers. They can tell you what the existing communication network is, who runs in what circles, who the workers are and who the slackers are. There are people there who already know the kinds of things that you need to learn, particularly when it comes to how to get certain things done in the church.

- **Larger community context** – It's a wise thing to study the community that the church is in. Does the membership represent the local community? Or do most of the members come in from long distance? Is there a good relationship with the community or a sour history? Are there community problems that your group could effectively address? Are there cultural barriers that would prevent you from ministering to them? One church I knew about was a Korean congregation, solidly planted in the middle of a Hispanic community. The Koreans drove from long distances to come to church. Would the Koreans be open to community outreach if they are not part of the Hispanic community?

- **Impediments to movement** – Find out if there's an organizational problem somewhere that would prevent you from implementing your strategy. For example, if most of your group are high-energy, 9-5 (or later!)

career workers in downtown Manhattan, welding these people together in a tight church community is going to be a major hurdle; they simply don't have the time. One youth worker I knew couldn't get his kids together on Friday nights because the parents didn't want yet another church function to drive them to.

This might sound as if you are spying on everyone in the church, but that's not the case at all. It's your job as the leader to know the situation thoroughly if you are going to help everyone in their tasks. The military knows that officers have to keep constant watch over the enlisted men because, without supervision, they tend to slow down and play instead of work. And keep in mind, also, that people are a bit shy about approaching those in authority – you will probably have to initiate the discussion and ask a few questions, because they probably won't be very forthcoming with much information.

Problems to solve

The main problem in any church is to get people *willing* to do what they are supposed to do. All churches have problems; but the only problem that can't be solved is if people don't want to do what is necessary.

It's true that God is sovereign, and he can and will do whatever he pleases. It's also true that nothing we do will merit a place in his Kingdom. And it's true that what he does is saving; our own efforts are auxiliary to his at best. We can't do what he can do.

But for every verse in the Bible that teaches us how important God's works are, there are a hundred verses that tell us we *must* do something or we are not going to get anywhere in his Kingdom. "Make every effort ..." "Examine yourselves ..." "He who perseveres to the end ..." "Continue to work out your salvation ..." "Be imitators of Christ ..." It is a fact that we have to *want God*. If that, then God will do the rest; if not that, then don't expect anything from him. "Your troops will be *willing* on your day of battle." (Psalm 110:3)

You can't motivate people to want God. Only the Spirit of God can change their hearts to that extent. But as the leader you can plow the ground, so to speak, to get it ready for the Spirit to work. You plow the field and plant the Seed, and the Spirit will hopefully make it grow.

The church runs on willing workers. Since it's a "voluntary" organization, you can't make them stay and do their part. Theoretically, however, it's *not* a voluntary organization: once you become a Christian, you are now God's slave (Romans 6:18) and obligated to serve him! Anybody who stands on his rights to do as he pleases doesn't deserve Heaven's reward. It's only in humility, gratitude, and obedience that we will experience God's blessings.

At any rate, there's only so much you can do, since this problem of motivation is not in your hands. But it *is* up to you to set the stage for people to meet God and get motivated; that takes planning and savvy. You can also stay alert for those who suddenly join the ranks with all their heart – it's those people you will want to train, equip, and put to work right away. Never waste the opportunity of a willing Christian. All they need is your leadership; they already want to serve the living God.

You are up against imposing problems if you want to motivate people. Even in the church, the members are amazingly resistant to doing what God commanded them to do. Your job is to effectively solve five seemingly insurmountable problems:

1. Teach people who don't want to learn

Rarely will a church member willingly sit down to study, even the Bible. If you can make it entertaining, they may spend a little time. But studying the Bible as if it's a textbook will be a chore to them. You can help things along if you can do the following:

- **Show holes in their understanding** – People don't like to discover serious flaws in their prim little world view. If you can show them that they believe a heresy, or their view of God is sadly out of touch with the Bible's teachings, or that they haven't come anywhere near satisfying the Bible's requirements for a holy life, they may just be more willing to hear what you have to say. For example, Jesus surprised us all when he calls our *attitude* towards others a prelude to murder.

> You have heard that it was said to the people long ago, 'Do not murder, and anyone who murders will be subject to judgment.' But I tell you that anyone who is angry with his brother will be subject to judgment. Again, anyone who says to his brother, 'Raca,' is answerable to the Sanhedrin. But anyone who says, 'You fool!' will be in danger of the fire of hell. (Matthew 5:21-22)

- **Bring out the richness in the Old Testament** – Almost nobody in today's church has a good grip on the Old Testament. I have gotten many a Christian turning the pages of the Old Testament when I showed them the Gospel in the story of Abraham, and the perfect organization of the church in David's story, and the key to conversion in Genesis 1. And when I can explain why Jesus took such a hard line against the Syro-Phoenician woman by using the book of Genesis, it makes people think that perhaps Paul was right – it's through the *Old* Testament that we learn the most about Christ and are saved! (2 Timothy 3:15)

- **Test for mastery** – This is a vital educational tool that no church I have ever seen is using today. What a shame. Pretty much every church relies on oral teaching, and the lessons go in one ear and out the other. And the next week nobody remembers what was taught the week before. Why are we doing this? Obviously it's not helping people remember anything! We can change everyone's attitude about learning the Bible if we would use the simple expedient of testing students in what they supposedly learned. At the very least, they will be so embarrassed about their casual attitude of learning God's Word that they will put more effort into it.

- **Set up battles to win** – The smart leader will take his troops out to a battle once in a while to give them the taste of victory. Not great battles, but fights that he knows they can win. The long, dull training sessions usually bore the troops; but put them in the middle of a fight to test their mettle, and they get positively excited about how all this training works. Suddenly it isn't boring anymore; they can see how relevant it is to their lives, when they see it in action.

I once taught a class of college students about the purpose of the Bible: the whole book is about God. Any sermon or lesson in the church has to tell us something about God or Christ to be Biblical and useful to us. About a year later, one of the students came back and told me that she attended some conference where a well-known speaker came to preach. While the others sitting around her loved the speaker, she was uncomfortable about him – she couldn't quite put her finger on what was wrong. Suddenly she realized that he wasn't saying anything about God! It was a man-centered religion, giving people nothing that would really help them spiritually. If my lesson didn't make much of an impression on her back in the classroom, the sudden illumination of its point in what this speaker was doing (or not doing!) was enough to convince her completely.

- **Expose the world's true nature** – Because of its importance in the Mission statement, one of the roles of the leader is to convince people to turn their backs on this world. Why would they want to go to Heaven if they are satisfied with staying here? So, use the Bible to reveal to them the truly ugly and poisonous nature of the world they so love. Once you show them how disgusting it is in God's sight, and how spiritually dangerous it is for anyone who wants to please God, you will find more of them willing to pack their bags and leave it. For example, who would want to live in a world like this?

> They have become filled with every kind of wickedness, evil, greed and depravity. They are full of envy, murder, strife, deceit and malice. They are gossips, slanderers, God-haters, insolent, arrogant and boastful; they invent ways of doing evil; they disobey their parents; they are senseless, faithless, heartless, ruthless. (Romans 1:29-31)

- **Select proper materials** – Sometimes the problem of motivation can be as simple as giving people only what they can handle. You have no doubt heard about exceptional students in public school who were bored stiff, because the teacher lowered the lesson to the level of the slowest student in the class. If you insist on writing your own version of "Christianity for dummies," only the dummies will be interested. The brighter students will go elsewhere. And conversely, if you throw Ph.D. work at spiritual infants, they will give up in despair and think Christianity is only for geniuses. You have to grade the material to the abilities of your students if you want to keep them interested and motivated. Remember the problem in Hebrews.

- **Connect knowledge with holiness** – Here is a vital avenue for motivating people. The Scripture is plain about the connection between knowledge and holiness:

> We have not stopped praying for you and asking God to fill you with the knowledge of his will through all spiritual wisdom and understanding. And we pray this in order that you may live a life worthy of the Lord and may please him in every

way: bearing fruit in every good work, growing in the knowledge of God. (Colossians 1:9-10)

You can't possibly live in a way pleasing to God if you don't know God, if you don't know what holiness is, if you don't know the requirements of the Law, if you don't know who Jesus is and what he does for his people – the list goes on. And be sure to point out the other side of that path – the people who end up in moral trouble are the ones who didn't bother to study the Bible.

2. Lead to Heaven those who want to stay here on earth

We may say that we want to go to Heaven, but when it comes down to it, we aren't going to give up this world so easily. Going to Heaven means leaving this world behind – and everything in it. As soon as we become Christians, God has ways of making that transfer from one world to the next very real, and it is usually distressing – he starts taking away our material possessions. But as Jesus said, only when the seed dies will the plant grow. If you want your church members to follow you to Heaven, you will have to work in these areas:

- **God-centered, Christ-centered hope** – Do what most ministries fail to do: focus on *God*. Show them the beauty, the power, the majesty, the wisdom of God. Dwell on his justice, his loving compassion, his forgiveness, his eternal nature. Study the stories in the Bible where he shows his complete control of every situation, no matter what man tried to do to stop him. The more appealing you make him to your hearers, the more willing they will be to go to Heaven with him instead of staying in this dark, disappointing world without him.

  > Praise be to the God and Father of our Lord Jesus Christ, who has blessed us in the Heavenly

realms with every spiritual blessing in Christ. (Ephesians 1:3)

- **Expose temptations of the world** – Because we are in a spiritual battle, the dangers are spiritual; and as a result they are difficult if not impossible to see. Use the Bible to expose them for what they are. The sweet pleasures of the world are often poisonous for the soul. As the Puritans used to say, gold will often weigh a person down to Hell. If you do your job well, your hearers will fear to touch anything in this world without first getting protection from God who saves his people. Paul talked about the love of money being the root of all evil; Jesus said that lust is the same as adultery; Samuel rebuked Saul and stripped him of his kingdom because of his lack of obedience to God. Warnings like these should not be taken lightly.

- **Take the heart & mind off this world** – One of the ways that the enemy keeps us firmly in his grip is to keep us busy with matters of this world. If he can throw things at us that make us fear him, we will submit to him; if he can serve up dish after dish of things that we enjoy, we will stay at his table. Keep the mind occupied with politics, or sports, or war, or the business world, and we won't have time for anything else – including church.

  So, your task as a church leader is to occupy their minds and hearts with God's world as much as possible. Deliberately schedule things to conflict with the world's events. Give them homework to do to keep them busy with spiritual matters. Have church-wide meetings during the week. You will have to interfere with their schedules if you want their attention; Christianity can't work if it's limited to one hour on Sunday morning!

- **Give up goods** – Jesus told us that it's impossible to serve both God and money. He knows our hearts; he knows what a strong hold our possessions have on us. Look at how far he got with the rich young ruler – the man turned away from following Christ because he wouldn't give up his wealth. (Here is a sobering lesson that motivation doesn't always happen in the church, not even in Christ's ministry!) You can't make people loosen their grip on their money, but you can set up situations where they have the opportunity to do so, if the Spirit leads them. For example, bring them into contact with the poor and needy. The Bible specifically tells us to do this. Start storing up spiritual treasures by giving away earthly ones.

> I tell you, use worldly wealth to gain friends for yourselves, so that when it is gone, you will be welcomed into eternal dwellings. (Luke 16:9)

- **Focus in prayer** – Prayer is the weathervane of the soul. It shows, better than most other things will, how you stand spiritually. As Paul said to do, "Set your minds on things above." (Colossians 3:2) Most of the prayer meetings that I've attended focus almost exclusively on "things below", not on things above. You, the leader of the group, need to change this immediately. Focus on God and his spiritual treasures when you pray. You may not know how to do that, but you can find plenty of help and counsel about prayer in the lives of the saints recorded in the Bible. Pray like that, and your church members will realize that you are living in, and longing for, a different world. Hopefully they will come to want the same world.

3. *Make more righteous those who think themselves OK*

One of the hardest things to convince people of is the *need* for a Savior. They willingly admit that they need a lot of things – money, friends, health, a good job, a nice house. But tell them that they are sinners, deep in sin, fatally corrupt in their hearts, and most probably you will have a war on your hands, not willing followers. They might admit to a little sin, but they don't want you calling them a spiritual criminal.

The problem is that they have to see themselves in that light, if they hope to be saved. Jesus didn't come to save the righteous, but sinners. We have committed a deep and fatal insult to our Creator, more profoundly fatal than we can know. That's why there's a Hell. God destroyed the world once because of man's innate sinfulness. To God, sin in any degree is an unfathomable abomination in his Kingdom and must be destroyed. The sacrifice of Christ ought to come close to convincing us how seriously God takes this issue of sin.

So, how are you going to convince people of their need for a Savior?

- **Plan for opposition** – Before we go any further here, you may as well know that this single issue is the most capable of stirring up violent opposition to your ministry. The point that you have to bring them to is a prostrate, humiliated fear of God the Judge and Lawgiver. The more you work with people, the more impossible that will seem; pride and rebellion are deep in the human heart and can only be cut out with the sharp edge of the Word in the Spirit's hand. (Hebrews 4:12-13) But when it happens, you will have a genuine conversion from sinner to saint, someone ready to be made into Christ's likeness. A drastic change is required, but you will have a battle on your hands until it's done.

- **Be specific about sins** – If you want to face people with their sin, you have to spell it out for them. It's not good enough to tell people that they are sinners. They will fill in the blank with whatever low-level "sin" they can think of. So use the Law of God to define sin; it was designed for that. Use Paul's teachings about how none of us have ever kept that Law. Use Jesus' expansion of the Law in the Sermon on the Mount;

don't let sinners escape from the true depth of the intent of the Law. Above all, don't use man's cultural and social standards as definitions of sin, because even the wicked can see through that. Stick to the Word. Its penetrating analysis of our hearts and actions is quite capable of convicting the guilty. Try the Prophets: their scathing analysis of the Israelites' hearts finds an uncomfortably similar target in our own hearts; we will hear their message again on Judgment Day.

- **Tie sins to suffering & defeat** – Since this world is God's creation, you can make a convincing case for the penalty of disobeying God. "The soul that sins shall die." "The wages of sin is death." Genesis 3 teaches us that death is a result of our sin. Sickness, wars, ignorance, family disasters, even accidents bring death and misery to millions around the world – as a direct result of sin. We are breaking God's creation laws, and the penalty will always be suffering. Again, Proverbs is an excellent study of the causes and effects of living in God's world: spiritual causes, physical effects.

- **Show reasons for humility** – Pride is probably the hardest sin to eradicate; God particularly hates it. It makes us think we are better than we are. It even separates us from God himself, making us feel self-sufficient. You would do well to strike at this independent spirit. Show people how powerless they really are, and the danger they are in when they ignore God. Show the results of their sin, the scope of their sin, God's attitude toward it, the damage it causes everyone around them. Plow the ground like this, and pray that the Spirit may humble them. If you can show them in the mirror what they truly look like as sinners, they won't feel so well about themselves. They will feel like the spiritually diseased persons they are and start looking around for spiritual medicine.

- **Offer a way of escape** – But don't leave convicted sinners at the door of the Temple without showing them the way in. There is a way in – by God's amazing mercy – but only for the sinner who brings the right sacrifice with him. The key here is to show them Christ *just when they need him*: when someone is truly in heartfelt agony over the sin in his heart, that's when the medicine will be most appreciated and used.

- **Train for walking with Jesus** – For those who have already made that transaction with the Savior, you will probably have to remind them over and over of the fact that they are still sinners. Conversion didn't make them perfect; it only brought them and Jesus together. There remains the process of *sanctification* – turning the legal status into reality. It's easy to show people how much there is yet to do: show them the perfect life of Christ, and encourage them with the point that they can quit working on their righteousness when they have become as perfect as Jesus is. That ought to set the bar high enough!

4. Discipline those who won't be led

It's always been a problem in groups, even in the military, of getting people to follow the leader. Though people understand this principle very well in the secular world (and for those who don't, leaders have ways of changing their attitudes!), for some reason they can't transfer that idea to the church. Here they feel that everyone is on the same level. It's true that there is no distinction between Christians, but it is *not* true that there is no need for leadership.

You can't make people follow you. But you can set up the situation in such a way that they come out the losers if they don't follow. You can make the cost of not obeying church leadership too high a price to pay.

- **Honor Christ as the Head** – This means that there is a hierarchy in his Body. We are *not* all equal as far as function goes. At the very least, none of us is allowed to do anything that Jesus hasn't specifically commanded. Just sticking to that rule would go a long way to straightening out church problems.

  Your job is to show people clearly that the church is not a democracy. Christ is the perfect King; he has no need of our votes or ideas. The checks and balances that a democratic society has formed to protect itself against tyranny are pointless in Christ's Kingdom. To think otherwise is to insult his wisdom and power and justice in how he has put together his Church. The only things we have accomplished over the years with our own brand of wisdom amounts to a moral and spiritual disaster. Why would he give any credence to our opinions?

  > You are my friends if you do what I command. (John 15:14)

  And since Jesus has everything planned down to the minutest detail, it only remains for us to carry out his will to the letter. Remember that the leadership in the church isn't doing anything on their own authority, not if they are faithful shepherds. They simply convey the will of Christ to the congregation; hence the heavy emphasis on teaching and preaching the Word of Christ to the congregation. There's simply no room here for opinions, or any deviation at all from Christ's revealed will.

- **Explain discipline** – Discipline seems to be a bad word for many people; it brings up images of punishment when they were children. But actually it's a lifesaver for Christians. The military understands its value very well. Recruits may hate it, but on the battlefield that discipline literally means the difference between victory and defeat. We will have more to say about discipline later, but here we will point out that you would do well to show the benefits of discipline, and the disasters that can happen when one isn't disciplined. Discipline can only happen, however, when everyone follows the leader. It can't happen apart from the group; everyone must be under the same discipline. "An army of one" is nonsense, as Patton once pointed out.

- **Promote team spirit** – The last point is related to this one. Our nature is such that we like to be part of a team; we don't like to be alone, nor do we like to follow someone when nobody else follows. You may as well use this fact and do what you can to create a team spirit. Since the church is supposed to be a community, do things to make a community happen. Build shared values, shared experiences, shared hopes. Connect the needy with those who can help. Coordinate the different levels of training so that all the members are on the same page. The stronger you can make that community, the more willing and ready they will be to follow you when the time comes.

- **Make an example of offenders and slackers** – In the modern church we have taken a *very* laid back approach to troublemakers. Since we don't want to offend anybody, and we certainly don't want them to leave (taking their money with them!), we hate to bring up the subject of how much trouble they are to the church. But think through that a minute: all that will do is encourage others to cause trouble too, since it's obvious they can get away with it. It also discourages those who are trying to do what is right, as if all their hard work and honesty weren't appreciated or required.

You would be further ahead if you would make an example of these problematic people and shame them in front of the group, as Jesus said to do.

> If he refuses to listen to them, tell it to the church; and if he refuses to listen even to the

church, treat him as you would a pagan or a tax collector. (Matthew 18:17)

Put their standing, their very membership, on the line. Make it plain that the group needs only those who are devoted to the cause, not those who are fighting against us. Threaten them with dismissal, and do it if necessary, to make the point that rebellion and trouble will not be tolerated in the ranks. This will actually have a wonderful effect on the whole group.

> Those who sin are to be rebuked publicly, so that the others may take warning. (1 Timothy 5:20)

Not only will you be sending a clear message to others who may have ideas of causing trouble, but you will gain the lasting respect of those who want the group to be whole and spiritually healthy. They will see that *someone* is willing to do what is necessary to that end.

5. Make more responsible those who don't want to work

Napoleon once said that if you don't keep after the troops, they *will* slide quickly into laziness and inactivity. It's a fact of life. The employee just doesn't have the same motivation to make the company succeed as the company's owner does.

The problem is that *there is so much to do.* Maybe you didn't realize this, but the parable of the talents gives us an idea of how much there is to do for the cause of the Kingdom. A single talent weighed over 65 lbs. – it was not a little coin. I think Jesus wanted to impress us with the huge scope of work lying before God's people, on both the individual as well as the church level. No wonder he was so hard on that person who did nothing with his talent!

- **Expose weak links** – One of the ways that the military cures a lazy recruit is to shame him in front of his buddies. In fact, at the early stage of the training, the fear of his buddies thinking less of him will motivate the recruit to keep up and not be the deadbeat who is holding everyone back.

But you have to be careful here. It's not the weak and helpless that you want to shame; it's the proud and arrogant who think they are something when they aren't. The lambs – you are responsible to carry them if necessary, until they grow and get strong enough to carry their own weight.

- **Create community** – In most churches the people on one side of the aisle have no idea what the people on the other side of the aisle are living through. Our modern society has created a social disaster; we live completely within our own social circles, with little to no contact with those outside. I guess most members expect the government, or the church leaders, to take care of those in need. It never occurs to them that *they* might be responsible for their neighbor.

It's going to be up to you, at first, to expose the problem areas in the church. You probably don't want to wave the charity cases around in public for fear of embarrassing them; but you can bring everyone into contact with each other (which is what is supposed to happen at church!) so that people will start waking up to those needs and their responsibilities. If church is simply an hour-long meeting on Sunday mornings, little to nothing will get done about the needs of God's people. You have to bring them into more frequent contact with each other – and it will take a lot of creativity to do that in our modern society.

- **Keep antennae up for spiritual gifts** – You are also, as the leader, responsible for staying alert and open to the spiritual gifts that the Lord has distributed in the group. He *has* given out gifts in the Church, you know – he's not negligent about his duties. Whatever your church will need is there already. What you have to do is discover it, develop and encourage it, and put it to work. Most people aren't aware of what they can do until you put them in a situation where their gifts are evident. But once you start assigning responsibilities to capable people, they will get self-motivated to keep up the good work.

- **Be specific in duties** – One reason that people aren't motivated to do anything in the church is that nobody actually spelled out anything that needs doing. Most preachers will hammer on the members' duty to "use their gifts," but they don't get specific about what those gifts are. And other preachers will challenge the members to get busy in the church and help out, but they are so insecure about allowing intruders into their "territory" that they actually take away the opportunity for church members to do anything. The result is that people don't know what's to be done, though you will often find them very willing. But you will have to work hard at making it plain to them and training them in how to do it.

- **Require accountability** – This is an extremely important step if you want to keep cohesion and coordination in the group. When you give someone a job to do, ask for a report on progress and results. When they know they have to *measure up*, they will take extra pains to do it right. Unsupervised work almost always ends up in disaster; not only do you have to make sure that it gets done right, but also the people doing it have to understand that it's for the benefit of the entire group. Everyone will be watching them. Use praise and discipline when necessary, and you will go a long way toward motivating people.

Key Elements to leadership

Leadership is a finely-tuned skill; you have to get people willing to follow you, yet do it in such a way that would please God. You can achieve both if you take care to do certain things:

- **Identify your program with Christianity** – What you are doing here is following Christ. Christianity is nothing less than learning and obeying the will of our Lord. If they want to call themselves Christians, if they want a real church, then *this* is what they must do. It's amazing what people turn church into if you don't keep bringing them back to Christ's definition of a church, and what he said is the life of faith.

- **Base it on the Word** – Be careful to base everything you do and teach on the Bible. First of all, you need a higher authority than yourself if you are going to convince people to follow you. Second, there's simply no way they can disagree with you when you show it to them in plain print. In other words, the Bible is the standard, the blueprint – and you are not making any of this up! So if they have a problem with all of this, it's with God and not you.

- **Do it yourself also; lead from the front** – Part of the success of a leader is if he will personally lead the troops into hardship, discipline, and danger. If he "leads" from the rear – if he tells people what to do, but is unwilling to do it himself – he will find rebellion on his hands in short order. Part of Paul's instructions to Timothy was to "be an example to the flock in speech, in life, in love, in faith, and in purity." (1 Timothy 4:12) Not only will this serve as instruction for them on how to do it, but it will encourage them that you also feel that you are a part of the group, and in just as much need of the objectives of the Mission as they are.

- **Trust the Lord's gifts** – The Lord gave spiritual gifts to his church to build it up in the faith, to help them achieve the Mission. You have certain gifts as the leader. Just remember that others have gifts as well, given to them by the Lord. So think this through: if you are capable because the Lord made you so, then others will also be capable of doing their job because the Lord makes them so. You don't need to run everything! And they will do their job just as well as you do yours. Many pastors can't delegate because 1) they want to run everything, and 2) they think that nobody else can do it as well as they can. That's a flat denial of the gifts and their Source.

General Patton once said that if you have capable subordinates, then tell them *what* to do, not *how* to do it. They will surprise you with what they come up with. People are inspired to do their best, and please their leaders over them, when they feel they are trusted. If they don't perform, then re-train them or get someone else for the job. Just don't micro-manage the whole church. That really tears down the spirit of the church.

PREPARATION AND TRAINING

The objective is always the Mission. This requires appropriate training and drill, unity, and buildup of supplies. The purpose of the Church is to become a fighting force, spiritually, so that everyone will follow the Lord into his new Kingdom. Daily operations need to reflect this Mission-oriented emphasis.

PREPARATION AND TRAINING

The day-to-day operations of a church should focus on training and preparation. This is a far cry from what most modern churches are doing; most of them would be incredulous and ask "Prepare for *what*?" Then when the battle comes, they lose badly and wonder why.

As a leader, your role will be to keep everybody on task and in first-rate shape. You will need that far-seeing vision that they don't have. You know what they still lack. And since very few people are self-disciplined, you will have to provide that encouragement and leadership to keep them to the task. Most people don't mind a leader over them so long as they know you are there for their well-being, and they can see that they are making progress under your leadership

There are fundamental skills that every Christian needs to survive spiritually in a hostile world. Far from being a matter of taking a course or two on the subject, getting these skills will take a lot of study and practice until we all get good at defending ourselves from the enemy, and attacking his strongholds to win captives. The duty of the leadership is …

> … to prepare God's people for works of service, so that the body of Christ may be built up until we all reach unity in the faith and in the knowledge of the Son of God and become mature, attaining to the whole measure of the fullness of Christ. (Ephesians 4:12-13)

The Mission

We covered some aspects of the Mission previously, but let's take a closer look at how the Mission will direct the daily operations of the church.

The church is involved in many things, but it has to be about the business of getting people saved and into Heaven, if it does nothing else. Fail here, and there's not much difference between you and a community club. The church has special resources to achieve this Mission. Nowhere else on earth will you find this kind of help, to achieve this particular goal. That's why it's a bad idea to "diversify" and let the church get involved in the kinds of activities that people can find somewhere else in the world. The Church can't do these secular activities as well as the world can anyway. Better to focus on what we do best; then there will be no mistake in the eyes of the community about what we are doing here. When someone needs salvation, here is where they will come.

- **There to serve** – Keep in mind that every believer is personally interested in the Mission. People are not in the church to serve you. I heard of a pastor once (he only said out loud what many pastors feel subconsciously!) that the goal is to get the church members serving the leaders. What a gross distortion of the purpose of a church.

    Your job as the leader is to facilitate the desire of every church member to reach Heaven. You know how to get there; you know what it will take; so you provide the atmosphere, the discipline, and the opportunities for them to reach their goal. They signed up to fight this fight of faith, and they are personally interested in the outcome. What they need from you is the leadership to help them succeed.

- **Spiritual hospital** – In light of what the Mission is, that makes the church a spiritual hospital. The idea is this: when someone walks into the church, whether newcomer or established member, he or she is declaring to the entire group that they are there for help with their sins, that they are ready and willing to change to conform to the Lord's will.

    This is *not* how the modern church thinks of itself. People come to be entertained, encouraged, comforted, praised, noticed by the public – anything but treated as a sinner! Again, in order to realistically work on the problem, people have to understand the profound spiritual dilemma they have gotten themselves into with their sin. Until they see how extensive, and how disastrous, and how fatal their sin really is, they will never take it seriously enough to turn it into a church project.

John Wesley, the famous eighteenth century preacher of England and founder of Methodism, organized his house churches on the basis of repentance and holiness. I don't know anybody in our day who would willingly join his groups, for the simple reason that one requirement was that everyone agreed to be minutely examined, every week, about the sins that they had committed. Yet he had people standing at the door waiting to join! In his day, people were so desperate to be saved that they agreed to join a church that was specially designed to save them from their sins.[8]

Everything in the church's work is to be focused on this issue of our sin. Everyone wants to go to Heaven, but the one thing preventing us from getting there is our sin. The root problem behind all the rest of the problems of the world, the one reason we have so much trouble getting along with others, is our sin. It all comes back to that. There is so much to be done here that it *will* be a full-time project in the church. Time to shed our other hobbies and get to work; there's little enough time to accomplish it.

> Put to death, therefore, whatever belongs to your earthly nature: sexual immorality, impurity, lust, evil desires and greed, which is idolatry. (Colossians 3:5)

---

[8] See the appendix "Wesley's Account of his Assemblies."

Preparation and Training

- **Real change** – We can't be satisfied to simply admit that we are sinners and then leave it at that. As James says, we have to change.

  > Anyone who listens to the Word but does not do what it says is like a man who looks at his face in a mirror and, after looking at himself, goes away and immediately forgets what he looks like. (James 1:23-24)

  The leadership can help here. You have to be specific about people's sins. *First*, you must teach about sin, specific sins, and how God feels about them. *Second*, you will have to face some people about their sins, particularly the open and gross sins that are unacceptable among God's people.

  > Do you not know that the wicked will not inherit the kingdom of God? Do not be deceived: Neither the sexually immoral nor idolaters nor adulterers nor male prostitutes nor homosexual offenders nor thieves nor the greedy nor drunkards nor slanderers nor swindlers will inherit the kingdom of God. (1 Corinthians 6:9-10)

  Third, while you are not responsible to follow people home and uncover their lifestyle under a magnifying glass, you will have to honestly deal with people who come to you asking for help. Keep reminding them of what is underneath and behind all of their problems. Faithfully keep bringing them back to the real problem, and you will be like the doctor who is simply trying to help his patient by telling him the truth.

- **The five pillars** – The five pillars of the church are organizational principles that make the Mission possible. David, a "man after God's own heart," reorganized the nation of Israel according to these principles. Jesus, the "son of David," formed his

Preparation and Training

church around them. You as the church leader are duty-bound to continue in the faith and make sure these pillars are in place. [9]

As we said before, rare is the church that has all five pillars in place. But I can't imagine achieving our Mission without them. Most (conservative) churches will have one or two, but almost never all five. Yet it's easy enough to be aware of, and implement, all five pillars.

They are specially designed to move people's hearts and minds out of this world and into the next. For that reason, you may experience trouble convincing some people of their necessity. Don't back down. Which of these five pillars can you do without and still call yourself a Christian? You may successfully float your ship for a few years with two or three of them, but even if you are missing only one, you are certain to experience some trouble or circumstance that will cause you to collapse, and you won't be able to prevent it. It's inevitable.

- **Focus to win** – I know that people tend to trivialize something, even the essential, when it's repeated over and over through the years. The same thing will happen to the Mission statement. Everyone may start out strong, but time and weariness and straying attention spans will lessen the urgency of the Mission to the point that people will forget about it, or turn it into a cliché that nobody is working on anymore. When there's no danger, everyone relaxes. Strange how a problem appears just when our attention strays for a few minutes. Somehow you have to keep everyone on task so that won't happen.

  This warning may help to keep people focused: remember that the enemy is waiting for your attention

---

[9] See the chapter "Self-Preparation" for the list.

to wander and for you to lower your guard. He has much more patience than you do. When you aren't on guard, and you are not ready on all sides, he will hit you in your unguarded spot and ruin an otherwise successful program.

> Be self-controlled and alert. Your enemy the devil prowls around like a roaring lion looking for someone to devour. (1 Peter 5:8)

- **Everyone's goal** – The goal, remember, is to bring everyone with you. "No one left behind." This project is, after all, something that we are all interested in. There's no such thing as the clergy-laity distinction. The leaders are guiding the entire church to their common objective: *everyone* has to cross that finish line. Holiness is the goal of all of us, not just the preachers.

  Remember too that one weak point in the ranks will endanger the entire group. If a single person is not taking the Mission seriously, that can have disastrous effects on the entire army. *That's* where the enemy will apply his full strength, and you will find out when it's too late that correcting that disaster will be almost impossible; you will have to retreat and re-group. Better to stay on top of things and make sure everyone is ready.

- **Quiet times for drill, preparation** – The average person looks for time off so that he can relax and enjoy himself. There are times for relaxation, but taking time off now and then isn't what usually happens. Usually people take the *whole* time off for play and pursuing their own interests. Little do they know that battle will soon start again, and they should have been using that quiet time for preparation. When you make the enemy retreat, you can be sure he's not wasting *his* time. So when the Lord gives his people an extended quiet time, he expects us to take advantage of the peace and quiet

Preparation and Training

and brush up on our skills. *We can't learn war in the heat of battle.* There's just too much going on, and things happen too quickly, to allow us the leisure of looking up things in the textbook while the bullets are flying. The times for study are the times between battles. Don't be lazy, and don't let the church get lazy, when you have those golden opportunities to get more training. The army that "rests on its laurels" and succumbs to laziness and gets flabby will be thoroughly beaten in the next battle.

Intelligence

Intelligence is that branch of the military that provides much-needed information to the leaders. Leaders have a different kind of job from the one that the soldiers in the ranks have. Leaders are concerned with schedules and planning, supply problems, assigning duties and training, troop movement, etc. For all of these responsibilities they need information, current and accurate and lots of it.

Set up your intelligence function in the church as soon as possible, and make sure it runs well. Set procedures right up front: who will be responsible to report to you? When will they give you reports? What will they tell you? What is it you are needing from them?

- **Progress reports** – Take the Mission seriously. The church's job is to help people get delivered of their sins. Keep your finger on this pulse, and make sure it's happening. If people aren't making any progress in this area, their claim to Christianity is empty. Either you have a lot of hypocrites on your hands, or they are like children – clueless and helpless, needing you to take them by the hand and help them accomplish this. The other task is to get them ready for Heaven: spiritually-minded, loving God, hating this immoral world, actively working on the Kingdom of Christ. This too is an essential goal, and you must make sure people are making progress here or their hope for Heaven will be empty.

Make sure your programs are working. Is your teaching hitting home? Are the people understanding what you are saying? Are your teachers effective? Are the spiritual gifts appearing and working in the group? All the gifts in the church are for a purpose, and you need to be constantly aware of any progress or problems in the system. If you don't keep an eye on all of this, who will?

One pastor used a unique device to keep informed about the success of his sermons: he had a "Pastor's class" *after* the main Sunday morning service. The purpose of the class was to see if anybody got the point of the sermon, as he intended it. It was so revealing to see people missing his point! It meant major changes in the way he delivered his sermons, so as to make them more effectively understood and applied. With their feedback, he could make his messages more pointed and easy to remember.

- **Communication up and down the chain** – The Marines believe that the leaders need to listen to the lower ranks. They believe in it so much that they take great pains not to alienate their subordinates with an attitude of pride or self-sufficiency. They promote an atmosphere of communication, information, and reliance on all involved. After all, since the leaders are usually in the office making the plans, how would they know what's going on in the barracks or, worse yet, out on the field of battle where the soldiers live and die? They have to get vital feedback from the people doing the work, to see if the plans they are making are reasonable and working.

Fortifications

The science of fortifications deals mainly with defense. Patton famously declared that he didn't believe in defense; he was only interested in offense and keeping the enemy in retreat! But even he had to admit that there are certain things that one has to keep safe from the enemy – which is in the realm of *defense*. These things include the non-combatants, the training schools, the supplies, the line of communication stretching from the front line back to our home base, the army itself when it's encamped, and so on. If you don't take measures to protect these things, then you are a terrible commander and should be fired from your position.

Our main defense is God himself. The Bible says this plainly in many places.

> Do not be afraid, Abram. I am your shield, your very great reward. (Genesis 15:1)

> The LORD is my rock, my fortress and my deliverer; my God is my rock, in whom I take refuge, my shield and the horn of my salvation. He is my stronghold, my refuge and my savior – from violent men you save me. (2 Samuel 22:2-3)

There is where we start for our defense system. In military science, the principle is that a fortress is equivalent to multiplying your manpower by six times; there's a lot of strength and safety in those big stones. In Christian military terms, the defensive power goes off the charts – there is no way an enemy can storm the gates of God's fortress. The only way you could possibly lose the battle is if you give up and open the gates.

- **Defense** – The purpose of defense is to protect your "soft underbelly" – the parts of your army that can be easily damaged by the enemy if exposed. Every army has them. You have to make sure the enemy can't get at them; otherwise he will hit you there, and cause no end of pain and suffering for your group.

Preparation and Training

For example, you have beginners in your camp, who are learning the basics of the faith. Make very sure you protect them from heresy, or any teaching that would throw them off balance. There are always wolves (*aka*, disgruntled troublemakers in the church) circling the group looking for the young and weak to attack with their destructive influence. You also have sinners who are trying to find hope and deliverance in Christ; you will no doubt have to protect these people from the Pharisees in the group who want to condemn them and get rid of them (see 1 Corinthians 12:23 on this). You have teaching materials for training everyone in the church – don't let it get infected with liberal theology. Make sure all your teachers are on target with your goals, and nobody is going to inject poison into the system.

In other words, find all your weak points – you have them – and take measures to protect them from the enemy's actions.

- **Stores** – An army moves on its belly, it has often been said; ignore this and you will soon have no army. The troops have to eat. In our case, our food is the Word of God, the Bread from Heaven, the pure milk of the Word. You can never have enough of the Bible in your church. Work to provide spiritual resource centers: equip your elders to be rich in the Word, your deacons to be gracious to the needy, the older members to be wise in counsel to the young.

In my first church assignment, when the system was in full bloom, we had Sunday School, the Sunday morning sermon, a Sunday evening sermon, a Bible study on Wednesday night, "Saturday Seminary" on Saturday mornings for those who wanted a deeper plunge into Biblical studies, and occasional multi-week seminars scattered over the weeknights. There was something for everyone and plenty of it. Considering the fact that

Preparation and Training

we had problems in other areas, this abundant supply of the Word is probably what kept us afloat far longer than one would have expected.

- **Armor of God** – Each person in the church has to have his or her own personal defensive system. Like a warrior going to battle, each of us has been given a shield, armor, sword, helmet – everything we will need to defend ourselves. The list is in Ephesians 6.

    > Stand firm then, with the belt of truth buckled around your waist, with the breastplate of righteousness in place, and with your feet fitted with the readiness that comes from the gospel of peace. In addition to all this, take up the shield of faith, with which you can extinguish all the flaming arrows of the evil one. Take the helmet of salvation and the sword of the Spirit, which is the word of God. And pray in the Spirit on all occasions with all kinds of prayers and requests. With this in mind, be alert and always keep on praying for all the saints. (Ephesians 6:14-18)

We surround ourselves with protective spiritual realities like a fortress, and rely in these means to keep the enemy at bay.

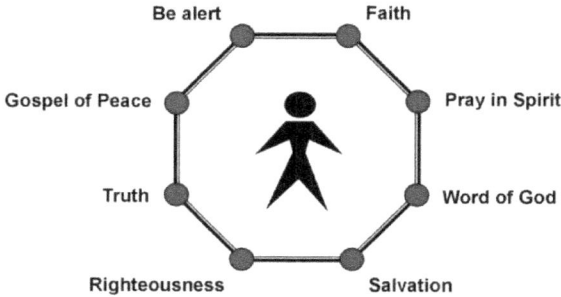

If we don't keep each defense point strong and in good working order, however, we create a weak point in our

Preparation and Training

defensive shield. The enemy is always looking for our weak points. Once he spots it (and he can find it sooner than you will probably be aware of it yourself) he will hit you *there* with his full force.

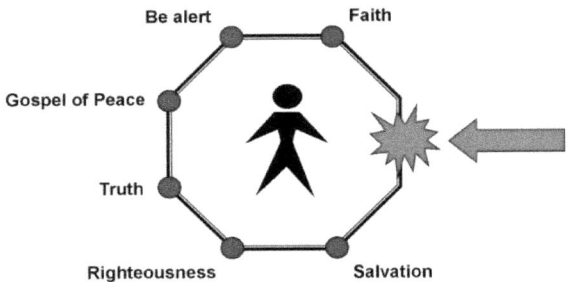

That's why it is vitally important to be constantly alert and on the defensive. You have to train daily, in all vital areas, if you hope to survive. You never know when or where the next attack might come.

And if the individual isn't careful about his own soul like this, not only will the enemy take him down, but now the church will have an open hole in the front line that will give the enemy a chance to get at the rest of us.

- **Backed up to the strong point** – Part of strategy involves deciding *where* to fight. A good commander is going to secure at least one side of his line on a strong point. In other words, if he can put his right or left edge up against a mountain, where the enemy can't get around him to attack on the flank, he has one less thing to worry about.

   Military training manuals include diagrams that teach tactical principles. For example, study the following diagram.

Preparation and Training

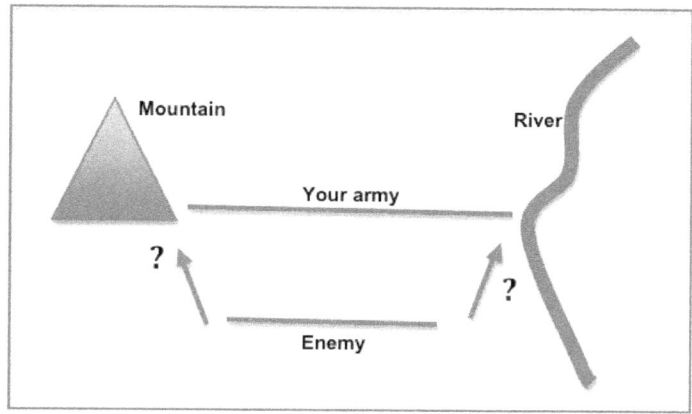

Strong flanks

Your army has two strong points: on your right flank (side) is a mountain; the enemy can't easily get around that. On your left flank is the river, which is also a serious obstacle to the enemy. He is forced to deal with you in your front, where you put all your strength. That's a strong position.

God has given us strong points to fall back on for security; there are many. One is the Bible; base everything you do and teach on that, and you will have a lot fewer problems on your hands. In our day it's the trend to doubt the wisdom and applicability of the Bible, as if it's a useless work of naïve primitives from thousands of years ago, hopelessly out of date. But if you give away the Bible like that, you have lost your standards of what truth is. Anything goes after that point. Of course there are various degrees of unbelief in the church; though a conservative church would never throw the Bible out, even they may sweep some doctrine under the rug and substitute their own wisdom for God's commands. Do that, and you are moving away from your strong point and opening yourself up to attack.

Preparation and Training

Another strong point is the church itself. The book of Acts makes it plain that Christians were not meant to fight alone, nor can they hope to achieve Heaven on their own. We are a Body – the Body of Christ. We need each other. As it says in Ecclesiastes, a cord of three strands is not quickly broken. Use this strength or lose the battle.

Search the Scripture for more strong points, and design your defense around them for ultimate security.

- **Built on the Rock** – The Bible calls Jesus the Rock for a good reason. He is unshakeable, he gives his people security and supplies in safety, and the enemy can't bring him down. Whoever "rests in Christ" gains all those advantages in life. God intended for us to go to Christ for that safety and rock-solid security.

    > Therefore everyone who hears these words of mine and puts them into practice is like a wise man who built his house on the rock. The rain came down, the streams rose, and the winds blew and beat against that house; yet it did not fall, because it had its foundation on the rock. (Matthew 7:24-25)

    He told us to take his counsel and follow his orders, and then we will weather the storms of life like a house build on a rock. Ignore him, and you will fail. He told us that there are going to be troubles in this world, but he has overcome all the world's troubles (John 16:33) – so stay with him. He has the words of life. He is the way to Heaven. He is the light of the world; remain in that light, and you won't have to walk in darkness. He is Bread from Heaven that we can survive on.

    That's just on an individual level. The church itself needs to remember that Jesus is the Lord of the church, the head of the body, the King – and our duty is to serve him, not do whatever pleases us. So find out what his

Preparation and Training

will is and do it. Base your church functions on that principle, and you can't lose.

- **Engineers** – The military uses engineers to build the fortifications. They are experts in security and fortresses. You will also have certain people who are good at this sort of thing. Put them to work. You have a lot of your own work to do, and you have to pass on some of these tasks to others who can take the load off your shoulders. You will have to train them, of course – not everyone is going to see at first the tremendous importance and scope of fortifications in the church. But get them started and keep them at it.

  Engineers are concerned with getting people from here to there. These are the administrators, the lesson planners, the program builders. They provide the structures that the church uses to enable people to plug into the system, get their training, and move out to battle. They build bridges to connect groups, they build walls to protect people from the enemy, they build roads so that everyone can move quickly as they carry out their assigned tasks. In other words, the engineers make it possible for others to do their part in the church.

- **Encampment rules** – When the army is in camp, either in training, resting, or between marches, the first thing to do is set up security around the camp. In camp the army is terribly vulnerable to the enemy. Everyone is tired, the arms are stacked up somewhere, people are standing in line for chow, officers are gathered together in meetings – it's the perfect time for the enemy to hit them. Woe to that commander who doesn't have a patrol always on the alert around the camp.

  This too is an element that the modern church almost never thinks about. Someone has to stay on the alert at all times. Someone has to "pray without ceasing." Someone has to watch out for dangerous elements aiming at weak points. You will be busy with the affairs of the church, and your eyes can't be everywhere at once. So you will have to assign patrols who will be on the lookout for enemy activity.

Self-appointed spies, however, are pretty much useless. They usually don't have the ability to read the situation correctly; they will be eager to bring you false information, but you need to refrain from taking them too seriously. There are plenty of gossips and back-stabbers in the church who are looking for any way to become more important in your eyes.

And your pickets also have to remember to bring news back to *you*, not start a fight on their own. You are in the position, and you have the authority, to make decisions on what to do and move resources to meet the need – they aren't. General Lee was forced into battle on bad ground at Gettysburg, because his forward patrol started shooting at the Yanks instead of getting back to him first. The result was that Lee lost the battle.

Discipline

Probably the single most important characteristic of a victorious army is its discipline. Discipline is a broad concept; punishment of crimes is only a minor aspect of it. We can summarize it by saying that *discipline is the ability of a group of people to move in unison and effectively engage the enemy*. The Prussian army under Frederick the Great was known all over Europe as the most disciplined army in existence, and was greatly feared by the enemy for that reason. All the preparation for achieving the Mission boils down to how well the church is disciplined.

Unfortunately this concept is lost on modern American churches. Church members usually take a civilian attitude toward discipline: they see no reason for giving up their freedom to do whatever they like, whenever they like, cause or no cause. So, when recruits enter the military, learning discipline is the first item on the agenda. The military's goal is to turn independent civilians into a fighting unit. It's not easy, and that's why the military has to be harsh in its methods. And discipline is a never-ending process; even among seasoned troops, you have to keep drilling them and keeping them in top condition. If you don't, the spirit of the group will start sagging, people get lazy and out of shape, they forget their lessons, and they are no longer alert and ready for action. You have to keep polishing the blade or it *will* rust.

We already discussed motivation. Basically the Spirit of God has to make people willing to accept discipline and fall into ranks. Once they are willing, the following is what you have to achieve in the church if you want an effective fighting force ready to send out on the Mission – and only discipline can get you there:

- **Accountability** – As we have seen already, the purpose of accountability is so that the leadership knows the current state of the group. And, during battle, the right things have to happen at the right times for success to happen. Therefore we don't require accountability so that a few can lord it over the many, as some disgruntled church members tend to think; it's for the survival and well-being of the whole group, and for successfully achieving the Mission.

    Everyone must understand how important this concept is. We all have our jobs to do, and we all have to report to someone. Getting people to accept this idea will take a great deal of mental discipline. There are leaders and followers, shepherds and sheep, teachers and learners, officers and members. We have to achieve a high level of proficiency in all areas of the church, and the leader is responsible to see that it happens. Reporting on the progress made in these areas is essential if the leader is to do his job of coordination and strategic planning well.

    Paul got progress reports on the churches that he planted or helped with in any way. So did Jesus.

> I am astonished that you are so quickly deserting the one who called you by the grace of Christ and are turning to a different gospel — which is really no gospel at all. Evidently some people are throwing you into confusion and are trying to pervert the gospel of Christ. (Galatians 1:6-7)

> On the way he asked them, "Who do people say I am?" They replied, "Some say John the Baptist; others say Elijah; and still others, one of the prophets." "But what about you?" he asked. "Who do you say I am?" Peter answered, "You are the Christ." (Mark 8:27-29)

Get progress reports on a continual basis. You have to be able to identify weak areas and take measures to strengthen them. You have to know the state of readiness of all parts of the church. When needed, you will have to move resources to areas of weakness, or to direct points of attack against the enemy – and pay attention to the results of those maneuvers. If nobody reports back to you, how will you know that anything is working? If some aspect of the church isn't working out well, it's up to you to fix it – but you have to know about it first.

This is why the Scripture lays great stress on "obeying your leaders" – because they are facilitators of the work of the church, and they need everyone's cooperation and accountability to do their job well.

- **Trimming whatever doesn't belong** – Napoleon revolutionized his army by cutting back on the supplies that each man had to carry on his back. He decided that he could leave much of that material in supply depots and move it up to the front line when necessary. This simple maneuver made the French army fearsome: it moved quickly, and it wasn't so worn out when it reached the battlefield.

Unfortunately today's churches are doing a lot that doesn't have anything to do with the Mission. Bazaars, picnics, sports events, music shows, psychological self-help sessions, political events, even such far-out functions as rug-cleaning services and cheerleading training! With all this and more going on, they don't have the energy nor the focus to accomplish the Mission.

There are a lot of other unnecessary activities going on that actually get in the way of the Mission. This confuses people about the true role of the church: for example, many people join the church so that their children will have fun things to do, when actually the youth should be working on their souls at church just like everyone else. The school and community is for fun; the church is for salvation. Martyn Lloyd-Jones, on arriving at his first church in Wales, saw how spiritually incompetent and useless the church was in the community, and within months had eliminated all functions that didn't directly pertain to preaching, teaching, prayer and spiritual training. The church people were upset at first, but soon after there was a community-wide revival in full swing and everyone was busy with *what the church alone is good at doing*. Then they understood the wisdom behind his house-cleaning. Those extra activities they had before were preventing spiritual growth.

- **Survival skills** – An army has to spend a lot of time out in the field, undergoing hardships, and it's constantly in danger from the enemy. A large part of its training focuses on surviving in difficult times and conditions. The church is also called upon to turn its members into survivors. Life will have just as much hardship for them as it was for the Israelites as they made their way through a hostile desert to the Promised Land.

Preparation and Training

We are a long way from being expert survivors. The modern church has turned into an entertainment center, complete with celebrities, music and video programs, demanding consumers, fun and games, and requirements so low that nobody is expected to do anything except have a good time. So when times get tough, members drop out and start coming apart emotionally and physically with nobody to help them.

Very soon I expect conditions to change in our culture. With the mounting financial and housing crises, immigration problems, the energy and water shortages, immorality and crime running rampant, the unbalanced international scene, the poor showing of the educational systems – these and many more problems are bound to change the American landscape. If anything, the church is in for some hard times at the hands of the wicked. It's the church's duty to prepare its members for trouble and persecution, for privation and suffering, for being a light and a fortress and an oasis in a dark world.

People won't like training for survival – it means setting aside fun and games and faithfully practicing spiritual drills. But the story of the ant is instructive here.

> Go to the ant, you sluggard; consider its ways and be wise! It has no commander, no overseer or ruler, yet it stores its provisions in summer and gathers its food at harvest. (Proverbs 6:6-8)

Necessary survival skills include a complete dependence on God for all things, fervent and effective prayer, community fellowship, willingness to let the world and its goods go, heart and minds on things above, testimony, a deep understanding of spiritual principles and how God works in this world, remaining in Christ for safety and following his path through the world, and so on.[10]

- **Standards** – Our modern church has set the standards for Christianity so low that anybody, including the wicked, can be card-carrying church members. An appalling example of this fact is when I found, on the Internet, ads for Christian theological seminaries specially designed for homosexuals. I honestly don't know how they put those two ideas together in their minds.

It's time to set the standards high again, where they belong. Discipline means doing your utmost to reach the goal. Making church so easy that it makes few or no demands on the members is going to make them despise the church. If you use the standards that the Bible sets, then you are going to end up with a smaller group to be sure, but they will be a fighting force to be reckoned with; they won't be wimps. The Marines, for example, call themselves "the few, the proud – the Marines." That's for good reason: of all the military services, theirs is reputedly the toughest training program. Remember that Gideon only needed 300 in his assault against the huge Midianite army.

What we teach has to be the Bible, no more and no less. We are not interested in what the world has to say, and we certainly don't adhere to their perverted opinions of the Bible. Righteousness – in other words, what constitutes an acceptable life in God's eyes – is perfection as the Law of God defines it. We do not change our rules according to current cultural standards. Church members are all responsible, as priests in God's house, to serve both God and man in all things, according to *agape* love. That means giving of themselves even if it hurts, because they truly care

---

[10] See the author's *A Manual for Spiritual Survival*.

about other members' well-being. Our behavior has to be "beyond reproach" in the community; they may not like us, but there won't be any misbehavior to accuse us of. And people who break the rules *will* change or be shown to the door.

- **Drills** – The science of drills is twofold: to build up fighting skills with our weapons, and to learn how to maneuver on the field as a single unit.

The church has weapons that can "break down strongholds." Our problem is that we don't know how to use them to do that. We usually turn to prayer, for example, only when nothing else works. I saw a Christian magazine once that had on the front cover a statement to the effect that, since their political hero didn't get elected in the national elections, they supposed it was time now to turn to prayer – as if it's the last resort when politics fail. That's pitiful. They are supposed to turn to prayer *first*, not last!

> Do not put your trust in princes, in mortal men, who cannot save. When their spirit departs, they return to the ground; on that very day their plans come to nothing. Blessed is he whose help is the God of Jacob, whose hope is in the LORD his God. (Psalm 146:3-5)

Prayer, the truth, the Spirit of God, the body of Christ, the wisdom of God, the Creator, the Redeemer, the Temple in Heaven – these are powerful forces that will change our society from the inside out, if we can just get a few church members to see the power in them. Worldly weapons will not make a peaceful, just and holy society; the church's weapons will. But it takes a lot of study, and a lot of training in their use, before we can make them work for us.

The other side of drills is the unified maneuvers of the whole group. You have no doubt seen a company of

Preparation and Training

recruits marching under the orders of a drill sergeant: left, right, left, right, left turn by twos ... the drilling goes on and on. The goal is a perfectly aligned group of individuals moving as one body: smoothly, efficiently, nobody out of line, everyone going to the same place at the same time. It's awe-inspiring. It's also tremendously important. A mob can only move sporadically, and perform hit-or-miss skirmishing. A drilled company can get to the front line at the same time and pour in a withering fire on the enemy, causing it to break and run.

When one army comes against another, we will be able to tell if it's been training for battle, just by the way it handles itself on the battlefield. Let's say that Army B (the typical church) launches an attack on its enemy.

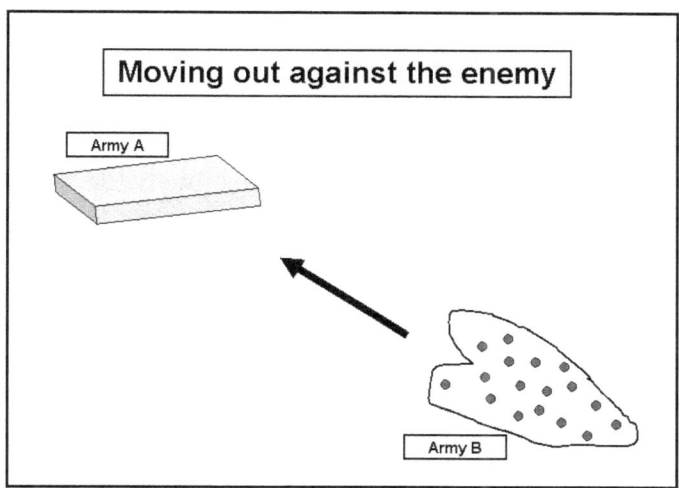

A mob attacks a disciplined enemy

Army B doesn't know what it's doing; it resembles an amorphous amoeba, spreading itself across the field. It hasn't been training for battle. It has unexpectedly encountered the enemy in the field; and even though there's been no formal training and nobody is really

Preparation and Training

leading this mob, everyone thinks that they can win the battle. Let's see what actually happens.

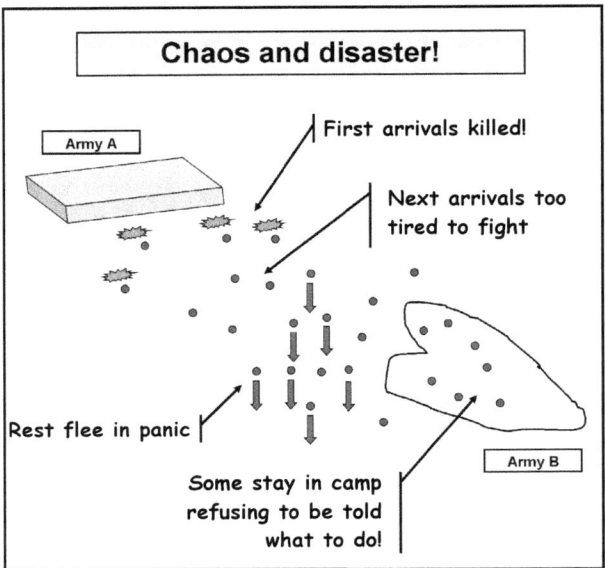

The mob loses the battle

When the fighting begins, we can see proofs of the lack of leadership, training and foresight. A few enterprising troops run across the field in their zeal and energy, and are easily cut down since they have no support around them. The slower troops behind them, as they are crossing the field, come too late and are too tired to give battle. The later ones see the slaughter ahead of them and turn and run away out of fear. There are even a few of the mob who refused to go out and fight; they are still back in camp rebelling against the whole idea!

Army A wins this battle easily, because Army B didn't know what it was doing. It wasn't even a close contest.

Preparation and Training

Now let's say that Army B learned its lesson (if there were any troops left after the fight!). They appointed experienced leaders who trained the troops day and night. Everyone learned their role in battle, how to use their equipment, what to do in tough situations. They learned how to march in step and unison. They have drilled so much that, even in the middle of bombs, bullets and bayonet charges, they keep their cool and do what they were trained to do.

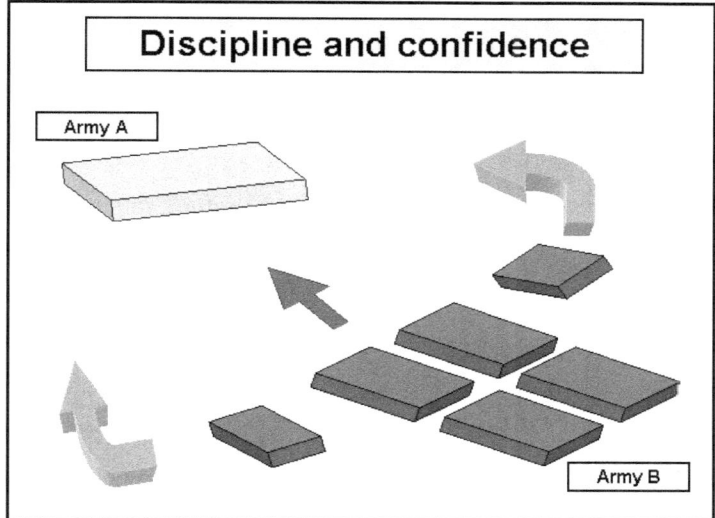

A well-disciplined army about to win

You can tell just by looking at how Army B approaches its enemy that it is well-trained, disciplined, and confident. The difference is a beautiful thing to behold. Army A is about to be surrounded and annihilated!

Would to God that churches would do this simple thing and train their members to work in unison. We need the same response to sin, the same love for the truth, everyone pitching in to help in times of trouble and need.

Preparation and Training

- **Dealing with problems** – One aspect, of course, of discipline is dealing with problems and the people who cause them. Not everyone is going to feel the same way about the Mission and its importance. The key here is to discern the kind of problem it really is and deal with it accordingly.

  Many people are believers, but they are just ignorant. They need discipline in their lives, even if they don't know it. Complainers, the lazy, the worldly, general all-around sinners fall into this category. You are going to have to confront them all about their misconceptions and keep them in the program. These are the people the Mission is designed for: the aim is to get them out of these bad habits and into the ranks of the Heaven-bound.

  Other people are not interested in the Mission. They will be harder to spot, because they are using the church for their own purposes (money, sex, power, etc. – all the sins of the world are in the church too, unfortunately). They are hypocrites who claim allegiance to Christ, but have no intention of changing their sinful ways to conform to his. Faithfully teaching the truth, and confronting them with their unacceptable behavior, will generally force them to seek shelter elsewhere instead of in your assembly where it's too hot for comfort.

  There will be a few wolves as well – be aware and ready for this.

  > Watch out for false prophets. They come to you in sheep's clothing, but inwardly they are ferocious wolves. By their fruit you will recognize them. (Matthew 7:15-16)

  > I know that after I leave, savage wolves will come in among you and will not spare the flock. (Acts 20:29)

These people are moved and motivated by the great Enemy of the church. They are out to hurt the sheep, destroy your authority, and stop progress on the Mission. Your job is to identify them, isolate them, and either destroy them (destroy their influence over the group) or get rid of them. If you make the mistake of trying to love these people, they will take advantage of your lax discipline and "spread the blood of the innocent in the streets of Jerusalem" behind your back.

The Lord made it plain in his Word how to deal with each kind of problem. Follow it to the letter; the safety and spirit of the group will depend on how faithfully you deal with problems. Discipline must be impartial, prompt, and thoroughgoing. God does not play favoritism.

> Do not be deceived: God cannot be mocked.
> A man reaps what he sows. (Galatians 6:7)

Logistics

As we have seen already, logistics is a vital part of military planning and operations. It has to do with supplies and how to get them where they are needed, when they are needed. By far the biggest expenditure in military energy and outlay is in the field of logistics. It's far more important than you may have thought. It's a complicated job and a responsible position. We have already mentioned a few things in regard to this subject, but let's focus now on the particulars.

- **Teachers** – These people are the personnel in charge of logistics.

  Jesus made it plain that his people must be fed: "Feed my sheep." "I am the Bread of Life." "This bread is my body." But we can't simply rely on church members to feed themselves. They are told to "feed on Christ," but most don't know how to do that, nor do they have the discipline to do it. Like children, they need someone to take care of them.

The teachers themselves have to be trained in how to bring the Word to church members. Just giving them a Sunday School quarterly isn't coming anywhere near to doing the job. Teachers of the Bible have to master the Bible; they will need a good deal of training in its history, its overall message, how the Old and New Testaments fit together, the great themes of the Bible, outlines, etc. Then they will need training in how best to present this material – different subjects require different presentations. If all this seems like a lot of work, it only highlights the warning in James about zealous but ignorant "volunteers" taking over an important function in the church.

> Not many of you should presume to be teachers, my brothers, because you know that we who teach will be judged more strictly. (James 3:1)

- **Everything necessary** – If you want your people to fight and fight well, every necessary item must be provided. Food, weapons, clothing, protective gear, ammunition, transportation, special equipment – the shopping list is huge. Cooks need everything necessary for feeding the troops in the field as well as back home at the base. The artillerymen need guns, transport, shells. The Air Force needs planes and ground crews. Marines need Navy ships to get them to the field of operations.

  In many wars in history, regiments and companies were assembled in local communities and drilled for the war. The problem was that many of them didn't have everything they would need for battle: they were often missing uniforms, guns, even shoes. Some companies went into winter battles with summer clothing; others

Preparation and Training

went to battle with no ammunition. The fault here lies at the feet of those in charge of logistics.

Your church, believe it or not, is in need of a great many things to operate well. You will need a logistics team to organize all of this and make sure nothing is lacking for anybody, no matter what their special requirements. Identify what everyone needs, what the elders need, what the deacons need, what the teachers need – everybody will look to you to provide specific resources necessary for their own jobs. And everyone in the church has to be skilled in the lessons of the Bible, the names and works and ways of God, prayer, testimony, the holy life, resisting the enemy, spiritual gifts, and so on. The training, therefore, must be extensive and balanced, lacking in no area.

- **Training materials** – People only remember about 10% of what they hear. That's not very good odds for getting them to learn, let alone remember, your lessons. You will have to give a lot of thought and energy to the materials you use to teach them.

  First, you obviously have a lot of ground to cover in the subjects to teach. Make an outline of all the different kinds of things they will have to learn. Different people and classes of people will need materials geared to what they are facing in life, and information that will help them master the spiritual skills that God requires of them. This will take a lot of study on your part.

  Second, be creative. Use outlines, pictures, paper, overheads, computer presentations – whatever resource you can to present the material. If necessary, find someone who is good at creative presentations – not just snazzy eye-candy, but materials that utilize the psychology of learning and how to best get it into the mind and heart.

Third, use good educational practices: repeat the important points over and over; keep the point of each lesson short and simple to remember; require feedback; test periodically to make sure it's getting through. You can find these kinds of principles discussed in educational training materials.

- **Training sessions** – Schedule regular sessions for everyone, from the elders down to the youngest children. The idea is to have an overall plan on what to teach, when to teach it, and to whom. Plus, it helps greatly if you can bring everyone through the same material (at different levels, of course) so that everyone feels a part of the overall Mission effort. Put it on paper, on a chart or in a spreadsheet, so that you can see the entire plan and make sure you are not missing anything. You will have to teach specific areas to different groups, schedule the subjects in the proper sequence, make things simpler for the younger (including the spiritually younger!) and deeper for the more advanced. Check off areas as they are covered.

- **Depots** – One area of logistics that you don't want to overlook is the fact that the army isn't going to be at the home base all the time. They will be on the move, out in the world, facing the enemy. They have to be fed during those times as well. The military uses "depots," or waypoints, to store up necessary supplies so that the army can use them to replenish along the way.

    It's your job – and your teachers' job – to make sure the church members have what they require during the week. You have no doubt heard many times the remark that people come back staggering into church on Wednesday night to get "recharged." That's your fault. They shouldn't be expected to go out for days at a time (many churches don't even have the Wednesday night meeting) surviving on what little they got on Sunday morning.

Preparation and Training

The early Puritan preachers used to visit their parishioners during the week and test them on the catechism. You can put books and pamphlets in their hands to read, along with tapes and CD's. Send out a weekly newsletter – just be sure to fill it up with spiritual food, not just birth announcements and upcoming picnic notices. Get weekly house meetings going. Give them homework to do, memory flash cards to work on. The goal here is to keep the Mission before them at *all times*, so that they stay focused – and advancing.

- **Gifts** – The spiritual gifts are listed in four places in the New Testament: Romans 12, 1 Corinthians 12, Ephesians 4, and 1 Peter 4. First of all, notice that they are clearly spelled out; beware of someone coming into your church and claiming a "gift" that isn't in this list. The Lord knows what we need better than we do.

  Second, a **spiritual gift** is designed to *make the Lord and his spiritual Kingdom more real and accessible to his people*. It fits in with the primary work of the Spirit: he reveals the things of God to us, and enables us to live in that spiritual world. And this fits right in with the Mission itself, because the gift helps us achieve our objective; it gives us the spiritual foundation and framework for our spiritual life.

  Finally, the spiritual gifts are for the entire church, not just for the individual. By God's design, we have to work together to achieve our objectives. Like a well-tuned sports team, the game doesn't depend on one player; we literally depend on the efforts of everyone on the team.

  But those spiritual gifts, so essential to the whole group, usually lie dormant beneath the surface. You will have to be the miner here and find them, dig them out, train them, and get them working in the church. Don't be like many small-minded, insecure pastors who can't let others participate – they want all the glory. If you do that, your church will fail on many fronts, and the Lord will eventually have to remove his lampstand from your group and you will be wasting your time in your ministry.

- **Lines of operations** – Remember that your group, and every person in it, needs to be able to get back to the safety of home base and supplies when they need them. You, or someone else assigned to the job, have to make sure everyone has a clear path back to God and the spiritual functions of the church.

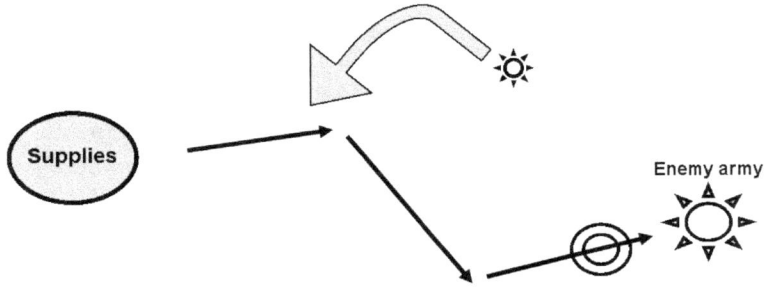

Lines of operation threatened by enemy

Study this diagram for a minute. Notice that your army – the circle – is a long way from home, having taken some turns along the way. You are finally facing the enemy, but unknown to you the enemy sent a small force out to attack from the rear. You are about to be cut off from your supply source! Be aware that this is the *first* place that an experienced enemy will strike you – this route back to safety. He can't hit our home base (the Lord is a fortress and a Rock that can't be moved), but he can hit us as we are trying to make our way back to it. So think through what "lines of operations" actually means in a church setting.

You have to keep communications open for everyone; the last thing you want is some poor soul stuck out in the terrors of the world with no contact with the church.

You can't afford to let someone starve out there, with no continuous supply of spiritual food. You can't have people doing their own thing and not getting back to you on a regular basis; they *will* be cut off from you eventually. You have to get the wounded back immediately; don't let them lie out there on the battlefield and die from neglect. And of course prayer, our all-important contact back to God, must be continuous, specific, and focused on the Mission, at all levels of the church.

Planning

Another responsibility of the leader of the church is planning. The military is always planning, even years ahead of time, for its maneuvers and battles. The general public only sees the story of the conflict itself in the news; what they don't see is the extensive, long-range, and complex planning process that went behind those dramatic few days on the battlefield.

Napoleon was a master planner. Once when he had shut himself in his office for days without coming out, his subordinates quietly entered the room to check up on him. He was on his stomach on the floor, lying on maps that covered the floor from wall to wall. He had sheaves of notes, and marks all over the maps. Amazingly, he was planning for specific battles in specific locations on the maps *three months ahead of time!* He planned exactly what he wanted to do – with an enemy that would unwittingly oblige him – down to the last detail. He even had specific plans for handling any situation that might change along the way (weather, supply problems, political events), as circumstances usually do, in order to bring his plan back to his overall schedule. He often explained his military success in that he left nothing to chance.

We know that only God knows the future, that in our business we can't predict the *specific* battles that everyone in the church will have to fight. "In his heart a man plans his course, but the LORD determines his steps." (Proverbs 16:9) But we do know the *kinds* of battles that can happen, and we can know (if we study) what the solutions are. There's no reason that we can't be prepared for whatever happens. In fact, it would be criminal for you as the leader if you aren't ready with the answers for when your people need them.

The point is that you must plan and prepare yourself so well that nothing surprises you; you can handle any problem or situation that comes up. And we are not talking about planning for picnics; plan for crises and real needs, the kinds of problems that would hinder the church in its spiritual work.

- **For changes** – Nothing stays the same in this changing world; you can count on that. So prepare for it.

  You will have people coming and going all the time in the church; there are always new people to feed and care for, and people leaving whom you were supposed to have trained and made ready for the world's challenges. So, give people all the essentials first, so that they will have them if they end up leaving before you get into deeper materials.

  You will have new teachers and leaders coming on board, and you will lose teachers and leaders (through sickness, troubles, moving, old age, etc.). The culture itself will change, bringing on new challenges as it invades the church from unpredicted directions. Enemies never tell you what they are up to – so expect all kinds of trouble from them at any time. Resources rise and fall with the social well-being of the group.

  You will have to meet these changes and more with wisdom and energy, and prepare ahead of time with actions and procedures that will meet the situation. Ideally you should write all of this down or it will overwhelm your memory, and you won't be able to bring back those good ideas of yours when you need them in a crisis.

- **For coordination of efforts** – Different branches of the military often have to coordinate their efforts in the

Preparation and Training

field for the greatest effect. Of course there's often rivalry between the branches, good-natured and not so good; but in times of war, everyone has to work out their differences and utilize each other's strengths for the war effort.

> I plead with Euodia and I plead with Syntyche to agree with each other in the Lord. Yes, and I ask you, loyal yokefellow, help these women who have contended at my side in the cause of the gospel, along with Clement and the rest of my fellow workers, whose names are in the book of life. (Philippians 4:2-3)

In times of peace, each department pretty much does its own thing and tolerates other departments. But in times of crisis and real need, the elders and deacons and teachers and church custodian and secretaries and nursery workers and bus drivers and evangelists and youth workers and parents and singles and married couples will have to work together if they want to see the church succeed. *You* are the facilitator to make sure this happens. Don't wait until the crisis happens, however, before working on a plan for this overwhelming task. Plan now for who will do what when, with whom, aiming for some reasonable goal that everyone can share in. It's certainly not going to happen on its own; it requires a well-prepared coordinator.

- **For tiered distribution** – Make intelligent use of the concept of the hierarchy of an organization. The purpose of a hierarchy is to distribute duties and responsibilities, so that everyone can stay busy and the whole job will get done.

The leaders at the top work on *strategy*, which is the big picture or over-all plan. Middle-level leaders work on *tactics*, the maneuvers and logistics involved to getting the troops to the field. The troops at the bottom of the hierarchy are the ones who actually go out and fight.

As you go down the hierarchical chain, people get more involved in carrying out the details of the plan. What this does is free you from having to micro-manage the entire church, and it gives the lower ranks lots of responsible work to do without your daily interference. So in your planning on what to do and when to do it, keep in mind that there's an impressive workforce waiting to carry out your plans in their own specific spheres. And if you are afraid they won't know how to do the right thing, then train them – avoid at all costs doing the work for them.

- **For flexibility** – The worst plans are the ones that don't get changed even when the circumstances change. The commander who inflexibly sticks to his original plan even though it doesn't fit the circumstances anymore deserves to be fired. The world changes; people change; needs change; the battle conditions change. Plans have to change also.

  Keep your ear to the ground. Watch what's going on. Keep your reconnaissance team busy, bringing back constant information on the conditions of the church and what people are doing and saying. Measure the church's progress spiritually and reshape your plan to bring it back into line with God's will. Be ready to change the plan at a moment's notice. Don't make the mistake of standing on your pride, or not wanting to appear as if you don't know what you are doing. It's not your fault that the world changes! The good commander will change what he's doing to keep winning the battle; it's only the ignorant man who will run the army off the edge of an unexpected cliff just to save his pride.

WAR PRINCIPLES

Like it or not, you have to be able to deal with the enemy; he will always be there fighting you. You have to know the enemy, maneuver your troops for battle, and apply the strategies and tactics that will be effective against the enemy.

WAR PRINCIPLES

When Moses led the Israelites out of Egypt, little did they know what was in store for them! They probably figured it would be an easy and quick trip to the Promised Land. What they discovered, however, was enemies lined up against them all the way. They also discovered that they would have to learn war in order to survive. Even when they arrived in Canaan, God deliberately left some of the pagans around instead of letting Joshua eliminate them all.

> He did this only to teach warfare to the descendants of the Israelites who had not had previous battle experience. (Judges 3:2)

Our Mission is to move into Heaven with God, with the righteousness of Christ. Unfortunately our enemies will not let us do this without a fierce battle – or rather a series of battles. War is inevitable; the question is whether we will be ready for the challenge, or give up and be destroyed.

Our Commander can't lose. He came particularly to engage our enemies and defeat them.

> Since the children have flesh and blood, he too shared in their humanity so that by his death he might destroy him who holds the power of death – that is, the devil. (Hebrews 2:14)

Once he frees us from the *power* of sin, it remains for us to follow him out of this world to be freed from its *presence* – but it will not be easy. So he teaches us war; use these war principles against your enemy and teach them to your church.

Be aware of spiritual enemies

Be aware that the enemy is not our next-door neighbor whom we don't like. Our enemies are those who would stop our progress in the Mission – the things that would prevent us from being saved and living with God. There is no more possibility of reconciling with our enemies than with a wasp that's loose in the room: someone has to die. So, even people who cause trouble in the church aren't the enemy in that deepest sense; they may be working for the enemy, and they may be lost in the end, but they may also be retrievable. Remember Jesus prayed for the Pharisees who nailed him to the cross.

- **The world** – *Do not love the world or anything in the world.* (1 John 2:15) The world is not our friend. The "world" that man has created is *not* what God first created! It is filled with specially designed pitfalls that will appeal to our lusts; this world is a playground for the wicked, for anybody who wants to follow roads away from God, and into self-glory and fulfilling one's lusts.

- **The flesh** – *The sinful mind is hostile to God. It does not submit to God's Law, nor can it do so. Those controlled by the sinful nature cannot please God.* (Romans 8:5-8) As if we needed more trouble, our very natures are to blame for the trouble we get into. We can't just blame the world, our parents, our genetic makeup, or the devil; we sin because we *want* to. As Eve discovered in the Garden, the temptations of the world appeal to our desires; so, using our desires as the standard, we take action on the temptation.

- **The devil** – *The devil ... was a murderer from the beginning, not holding to the truth, for there is no truth in him. When he lies, he speaks his native language, for he is a liar and the father of lies.* (John 8:44) The plot thickens, as most stories do, with the introduction of the arch-villain. Not that we can blame him for our sins; we are still guilty and fully responsible. But it sure doesn't help matters that we have such a formidable and ruthless opponent who is determined to destroy us – and he knows all too well how to do that. The devil is a master of lies and deceit. Satan's

War Principles

main method is to lie to us, to deceive us and get us to believe anything other than the truth of God. Then we willingly walk into a trap and get destroyed.

All three of these enemies must be destroyed, if we want to enter Heaven on God's terms. It has to be all-out war. This is how to carry out that war.

- **Identify the true enemy** – The first step in a war is to identify your enemy. That's not hard on the national scene; but on the church level, it can be amazingly difficult – simply because our enemies hide themselves.

  > And no wonder, for Satan himself masquerades as an angel of light. It is not surprising, then, if his servants masquerade as servants of righteousness. (2 Corinthians 11:14-15)

  True to war principles, the enemy uses strategy – hiding his real intentions, his movements, his resources, until the time comes to strike you at the worst time and place. Jesus showed deep wisdom and insight in being able to identify the enemy at work. For example, he singled out his own disciple Peter as being a dupe for the enemy:

  > Jesus turned and said to Peter, "Get behind me, Satan! You are a stumbling block to me; you do not have in mind the things of God, but the things of men." (Matthew 16:23)

  The reason Jesus could smell the presence of the enemy is because he knew their ways and their goals. And he didn't hesitate to name them; it's vital to be willing to call a spade a spade, so to speak, in the work of the church. For example, I wish people would name Liberal Theology for what it is – heresy, destructive of the church, a poison of the mind and heart that has deceived and destroyed the work of the Kingdom for the last 200 plus years. Naming the enemy is the first step to destroying him: it brings him out, and makes him easy for everyone to see. Paul didn't hesitate to identify a heretic.

> For such men are false apostles, deceitful workmen, masquerading as apostles of Christ ... Their end will be what their actions deserve. (2 Corinthians 11:13,15)

It's not mercy but cowardice that holds pastors back from so clearly identifying the enemy. Under the guise of "love," they would have us sweep problems under the rug and put things off till later, hoping they will go away. They will *not* go away; warriors bent on your destruction never do. They are hoping that *you* will take the spotlight off *them* so that they can work in darkness and secrecy!

Our three enemies are destroying our culture and our church. It's time to deal with them summarily.

- **Recognize dupes and traitors** – One particularly vicious method that our enemies have is to enlist helpers to work in our own ranks. It's bad enough to be up against enemies of a spiritual nature, because it's difficult to identify them and make them clearly seen by all the troops. But when the enemy enlists our own soldiers for his cause, it's very difficult to keep the church unified and on-task. It rips up the work of the church from within – a prime tactic and opportunity that is so prized in warfare. Within our own ranks we have someone shooting our troops in the back.

Again, you must be on top of this. It's perhaps more destructive of the church and its work than a direct confrontation on the battlefield. It destroys our will to fight; it destroys the spirit of the group; it confuses everyone about the Mission itself. For example, when David was forced into leaving Jerusalem while his son Absalom made a bid for power, David's counselor

War Principles

Ahithophel turned traitor and told Absalom how to destroy his father. (2 Samuel 16-17) The whole country was on the verge of disintegration, and now men once loyal to David were turning against him.

> Even my close friend, whom I trusted, he who shared my bread, has lifted up his heel against me. (Psalm 41:9)

Remember what the true enemy is and how he fights. Church members who fall prey to the sins of the flesh, the temptations of the world, and the lies of the enemy are actually changing uniforms and helping the enemy destroy the church from within. Look at it in that light if you really want to understand what's going on and how serious it is. If you turn a blind eye to these destructive forces, for whatever reason, you will be responsible for the church's defeat.

- **Deal summarily with them** – Jesus didn't hesitate to call out the enemy when he saw him. Neither should we.

> You snakes! You brood of vipers! How will you escape being condemned to Hell? (Matthew 23:33)

Don't let friendship or personal loyalties get in the way of your duty. Don't wait on the pretext that perhaps you might be wrong about someone. Deal with it immediately.

Of course you should be totally familiar with your enemy so that you can do this well. Many church leaders are so ignorant of the true enemy and his methods that they shoot at the wrong "enemy" – another church down the street, a political candidate, a church member they don't like, a social or cultural custom. So while they are busy fighting a useless war against a straw man, the real enemy is having a field-day right under his nose, destroying the souls of those under his charge.

Speed and courage are two essentials in warfare that you must utilize, or you will lose battles to an enemy who will most certainly use them against you. You may have only one opportunity to deal with a serious problem; don't put it off. And pray that the Lord will give you wisdom.

Organization

Hopefully you have organized the church in peacetime so that it will be immediately ready to swing into war mode, without confusion or hesitation. A well-trained army is always ready to go to war with a minimum of trouble. Many a church, however, has been caught unawares in the time of need: they didn't think war preparation was important, and the war, when it came (not *if* but *when*!) found them totally unprepared. They deserved the loss they experienced.

When it's time to fight, it's up to you, the leader, to get things going. Probably most of your church members have never faced the enemy like this. They will need your motivation; they will need orders to get busy with their special jobs. They will need directions on what to do and where to go. You have the task of getting this organization in place on the way to the battlefield, and arranging the different elements for battle. *You* have to lead here.

- **Assignments and specialties** – People may have trained diligently in their gifts, but they don't necessarily know what it's like to use them against real enemies and in real crises. Learning the lessons in the classroom is one thing; doing them in a dangerous situation, when someone's life is at stake, is quite another. Besides, it's one of your jobs as the leader to coordinate the different forces – you have to place them; you have to send them into battle at the right time.

For example, your teachers will have to come up with the truth, and the right truths, to equip students in the middle of a secular, God-hating, and immoral educational system. Put the older women (as the Bible specifically instructs us to do – Titus 2:3-4) in charge of teaching and leading the younger women in their household and family tasks. Make sure the poor in the church are taken care of (James 1:27); they are the first target of the cults who know how to pick up dissatisfied church members. When the battle starts (keep alert for the temptations of the world, the weakness of the flesh, and the lies of the enemy) assign the proper team to the job immediately.

- **Accountability** – During battle the leader *must* know what's going on. He watches over the battle and coordinates movement and resources. While others are fighting, he is thinking and planning. It's his mind against the enemy commander's mind. The only way he can do his job well is if there is strict accountability in the ranks. People have to communicate; people have to follow orders and report back on the results.

  The main reason that the average church member won't communicate with the leaders is that they don't like being led; they often accuse leaders of "lording it over them." But that's a childish complaint: it's both missing the point and destructive of the accomplishment of the Mission. The leader is not "lording it over his people;" he's coordinating a battle. They have no right to make his job more difficult. There will be little or no time for dealing with deserters and rebels in the ranks when the battle is raging; but when people act so childishly, they should be dealt with severely after the battle is over – their ignorance may have swayed the battle over to the enemy's advantage and put the whole church at risk. In the military, deserters are shot for their aid to the enemy.

War Principles

- **Command and Control** – In military parlance this is known as C2. As soon as the battle starts, the general assigns a subordinate with a team to take up a good position on the battlefield, and gives them complete control and authority over the situation. All information goes to them; they study the situation and make the decisions. They are always there watching the battle, and the responsibility of leadership rests on them alone. Of course the general is always listening in.

  This solves two problems: *first*, instead of having a lot of chiefs in charge, there is one person in charge. A plurality of heads during a battle is a sure recipe for disaster. Pride, different perspectives and training, having information that the other person doesn't have – these problems and more will inevitably cause conflict among the leaders just when you need decisive action. An average leader taking decisive action is better than two great leaders who can't agree on what to do. Paul, for example, sent Epaphroditus to the Philippian church to take care of matters there in Paul's absence.

  Second, everyone knows where to send information to and whom to get orders from. The lines of communication to C2 are clearly drawn and operate quickly and efficiently, which is critical in a battle.

  The pastor may or may not want to head up that C2 team during a battle. In many situations, especially if it's a small church or a crucial issue, he will probably be the best man for the job: he knows his resources better than the others, and his authority carries the most weight at a time when it's critical that people respect the authority. On the other hand, if the pastor decides to give the job to someone else, he has to keep his hands off the situation and let the C2 team do its job. Interfering with their job will insure failure, since you

War Principles

will be confusing the troops and dividing loyalties just at a time when you don't want disunity in the ranks.[11]

- **Assessment functions** – During a battle the C2 team is always studying the situation. Don't take as your war model these movies that focus on the guy doing the shooting. He actually knows very little about what is going on; so many times in battle, the ordinary troops have no idea of who is winning until they read about it later in the newspapers!

  Back at headquarters the leadership team is busy night and day, non-stop, poring over maps, checking the weather reports, making sure the logistics team is supplying the troops, reading the reconnaissance reports, tracking the enemy's movements, assessing the results of the army's maneuvers and re-shaping the plan to conform to the battlefield's ever-changing conditions. Aides are running in and out all the time with information and orders. It's very much an intellectual business; they are literally the brains of the army.

  Perhaps here is why many churches lose their battles against the enemy. Leaders don't set up shop to study the situation, measure the progress, follow the enemy's movements and tactics, and change the plans to fit the changing circumstances. They have to go into *assessment mode*: make a deliberate effort to lay the situation out on the table, discuss it with aides for their counsel and information, break the problem down into manageable pieces, send the necessary resources into the battle at the right time, and get reports back on the progress so that the leader can take further measures.

---

[11] To show you how much influence a pastor has, it's often necessary for a retiring pastor to find another church to attend instead of staying in the church he worked in for so many years. The members there are too loyal to him to switch loyalties to the new pastor, and the new pastor simply can't get the cooperation he needs to make his position work.

By taking an analytical approach during battle, you are putting yourself in a position to wage war intelligently instead of reacting to troubles blindly and emotionally.

Assessment in the church means taking tests and measures to see how much is being learned, getting reports on spiritual growth (or the lack of it), the status and training levels of the staff, and whatever other measures you can devise to take the spiritual pulse of the operations. With this information you can decide how successful (or unsuccessful) your program is and act accordingly.

Battlefield problems

Good commanders know that their plans will start falling apart as soon as the battle starts. You are up against an intelligent enemy, with a will of his own, exerting his energy and plans against yours, trying to out-think and out-maneuver you.

The question isn't whether you will have problems, but how serious they will be and how quickly they will cause your plans to change. Good preparation will keep your plan and army moving long enough to stay in control of the situation; bad or no preparation will cause you to fail immediately.

You can't afford to wait until you have problems before you deal with them. You have to develop procedures for potential problems and then apply those procedures quickly when they come up. Consider them as mines buried in the highway: they may surprise you, but get a trained team working on removing the mines quickly as the army marches forward; you don't want the entire army held up over something that should be dispatched quickly.

- **Weariness** – Even the best-trained troops get worn out after a day or two of intensive fighting. It's human nature; it's a limitation of our flesh and spirit. So, plan for it. Watch for weariness, and take measures to deal with it. Give people a rest when they need it. Move in other troops to take the load for a while. Refresh your troops with "a table set for me in the midst of my enemies" (Psalm 23) – prayer, the Word, fellowship, a view of Heaven, the glories of God's world.

- **Protracted struggles** – Some battles go on and on. Instead of a quick victory (or at least a quick defeat!) it can take months or years to reach our objective. In World War I, some "battles" (like Passchendaele and Verdun and the Somme) extended over almost a year and cost millions of casualties – an unimaginable concept to armies that were used to finishing a battle in a day or two.

  Battles like these are frustrating, costly, and demoralizing. Keeping the troops on task when there is no end in sight is one of the hardest things a leader has to face. *It is then that the will of the leader carries the army*. As Churchill once said, "Never, never, *never* give up!" Facing a determined enemy, with mounting problems in your own group (complaints, weariness, casualties, even insurrection and rebellion), it is only the leader's will that keeps the church going. The Lord never gave you permission to surrender to the enemy. Your task is to get these people to their objective or die trying. Moses spent forty years leading Israel to the Promised Land!

- **Defeats** – It's a rare leader who never loses. Some have come close: Napoleon won almost all of his battles, and the Roman general Scipio won all of his, according to the records. But you probably won't.

  The important thing to remember is that defeat is not the end. Someone once said about the British that they usually lose all the battles in their wars except the last one. That's high praise: a dogged persistence and refusing to give up.

See the defeat for what it is: a chance to learn. Frederick the Great considered defeats to be his most effective learning tool. Find out what happened, why it happened, and what you (or others) should have done. Change your training or logistics system to address that problem better in the future. Be open with the church members – admit your mistakes, and present solutions to address those mistakes that they can see will be effective. That will give them more confidence in you, interestingly enough, knowing that you know what to do to fix mistakes and have the courage and humility to face your shortcomings.

Make that defeat costly to the enemy; make him respect you as a worthy opponent and nobody to be trifled with. Even if you lose, make him wish he hadn't tangled with you and your church! He will probably back away and leave you alone long enough for you to mount a counter-attack against him.

The Scripture says that if we lose, it is often God teaching us necessary lessons the hard way. The church shouldn't be losing its battles; it's following a divine Commander who can't lose. But sometimes, the Bible says, he will refuse to go out with our armies.

> But now you have rejected and humbled us;
> you no longer go out with our armies. You made
> us retreat before the enemy, and our adversaries
> have plundered us. (Psalm 44:9-10)

Perhaps we haven't been following his lead, or listening to his counsel. Perhaps we aren't relying on his weapons, and we have put our hope in our own wisdom and strength. Perhaps we have become lazy and apathetic to the cause. Whatever the reason, a defeat should prompt us to do some soul-searching; something is wrong spiritually. For example, when Joshua lost his second battle in the Promised Land, he knew something was seriously wrong; God had promised him victories all the way. A little research brought out the problem in Achan's greed. (Joshua 7)

- **Barriers from the enemy** – A savvy enemy is going to put barriers in our way: felled trees, torn-up railroad tracks, burned barns and fields. And the enemies of the church will never fail to throw obstacles in our way as we fight to achieve the Mission. Look at obstacles for what they are: the enemy's attempt to divert you from the Mission.

> Woe to the world because of the things that cause people to sin! Such things must come, but woe to the man through whom they come! (Matthew 18:7)

These barriers are going to be unexpected and time-consuming. The goal here is to *stay focused on the Mission*, and deal with each obstacle that comes up quickly and efficiently. Obstacles can come from all over the map: people's conflicting schedules, financial crises, loss of teachers for whatever reason, squabbles between team members, community issues, cliques, heresy issues, immorality, and so on. We have very creative and persistent enemies.

Problems are a fact of life. Your job is to solve the problems as they come up, not get thrown off-balance by them. The Lord will always have a solution for the problems. Paul went through tremendous hardship, but he persevered in his task.

> I know what it is to be in need, and I know what it is to have plenty. I have learned the secret of being content in any and every situation, whether well fed or hungry, whether living in plenty or in want. I can do everything through him who gives me strength. (Philippians 4:12-13)

> No temptation has seized you except what is common to man. And God is faithful; he will not let you be tempted beyond what you can bear. But when you are tempted, he will also provide a way out so that you can stand up under it. (1 Corinthians 10:13)

- **Friction** – Friction is a military concept. It refers to the fact that, though you may think your church is a well-oiled machine, you will find out otherwise. As a battle emerges, you are going to find people who suddenly can't work with each other. You are going to discover deficient supply lines. You will see confusion in supposedly well-trained leaders and followers. What you thought was going to work out well turns out to be machine with scraping edges, an organization that can slowly grind to a halt if you don't take care of those rough edges grating against each other.

  Friction is always going to happen. There is no perfect organization on earth, no perfect church. And we have a clever enemy who is always looking for our weak points and throwing sand in our tank tracks and dirt in our eyes – which uncovers areas in our organization that need revamping or fine-tuning.

  The trick is to fix things while you are on the move, and that's not easy. It takes a capable leader to smooth out the road ahead of a marching army so that it doesn't get held up or diverted. But we have a few tools in our toolbox to make the wheels run more smoothly when the friction happens. For example:

  > Hatred stirs up dissension, but love covers over all wrongs. (Proverbs 10:12)

  > A gentle answer turns away wrath, but a harsh word stirs up anger. (Proverbs 15:1)

> Better a patient man than a warrior, a man who controls his temper than one who takes a city. (Proverbs 16:32)

In fact, a lot of the "oil" that eliminates the points of friction in a group, and its progress on the battlefield, is found in the fruits of the Spirit.

> But the fruit of the Spirit is love, joy, peace, patience, kindness, goodness, faithfulness, gentleness and self-control. (Galatians 5:22-23)

People with these personality characteristics are going to work well with each other.

- **Fog** – Another military concept, fog refers to the fact that it's often so difficult to see what's going on in the middle of a battle. Not only will the troops themselves struggle blindly in smoke and fire and sometimes darkness, the leaders back at HQ will too often be in the dark about what's happening on all points of the front line.

You have to be able to see, but the simple fact is that you *won't* see everything that's going on. Count on that. In fact, it's the stated aim of the enemy to keep you in the dark. The less you can see, the less you know, the better the chance that you will make a serious mistake and give the battle to the enemy.

Leaders have to be able to make decisions based on faulty or missing information; wartime never allows perfect information. You have to be able to see through the enemy's lies and misinformation; you have to be able to fill in the blanks when you know you are not getting all the data. You have to be good at assessing the situation correctly with only a few facts.

Here is where your previous rigorous training and study comes to play. If you learned the principles well, and if you have given them a lot of thought and practiced

War Principles

them over and over in artificial scenarios, you have a better chance of recognizing a few key pieces of those lessons in the confusing situation that you are in now. You already have all the answers you will need for church work in the Word. The question is this – can you recognize where to apply the correct solution to the need at hand?

Following is a typical diagram showing a tactical situation that you would see on a whiteboard in a military classroom.

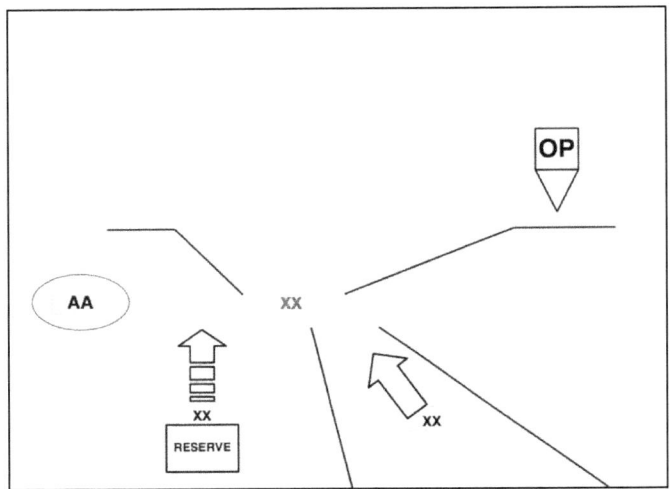

All that it shows us is a method of moving troops to meet the enemy; it's stripped down to the conceptual level. This is easy enough to learn, but it's also easy to never think beyond the bare conceptual diagram.

Here is a picture of a landscape.

War Principles

Although this is familiar to us as the real world, the problem comes in when we fail to merge the real world with the military diagram that we thought we had learned back in the classroom. If we actually merge the two, it turns out that this supposedly familiar landscape is a perfect example of the tactic we learned.

Now that we see them together, the thing is obvious. But it takes a trained mind to merge the two – to put the landscape with the right diagram. *That* is what is so difficult to do in the middle of battle.

So, we can learn the concepts of spiritual warfare in the Bible; yet out in the real world and the problem situations that we live in, we too often fail to connect the problem with the solution that we learned in class. That ability to merge the two does not come naturally! It's the result of discipline, study, practice, failing and trying again, until it becomes second nature.

Never forget, however, that even though we struggle with fog and darkness, we have an asset specially designed to shine the way for us.

> Let him who walks in the dark, who has no light, trust in the name of the LORD and rely on his God. (Isaiah 50:10)

That means that you trust God to guide you even though you don't have all the answers; it means to obey his commands to the letter, with no deviation, and he will guide your obedient steps even if you don't understand how success could come in this situation.

- **Shortages** – In earthly armies there is always a shortage problem. Patton had to stop his army in its victorious march into Germany because he ran out of gas. Interestingly, God's armies don't have that problem. Our supplies are infinite, and free for the asking, as much as we need.

  But we do have *apparent* shortages. As in any human endeavor, the spirit is willing but the flesh is weak. Teachers may not have much depth of understanding of the Word. Pastors can't deal with all aspects of the church – there's just not enough time and energy to go around. There may not be anybody in the group who is trained and skilled to be an evangelist. So, what do we do when we run to the end of man's limitations? We wait on the Lord. He is faithful, and if he withholds some resource for some reason, we have to be patient and keep to the task. He will give us what we need at the proper time. The story of the persistent widow (Luke 18) teaches that. Christ is, after all, the Commander-in-Chief, and he knows what he's doing. Apparent shortages aren't necessarily as fatal as we often make them out to be – not in the hands of the One who can feed thousands from a few loaves of bread.

One thing you *must not do* is turn to volunteerism. Many churches, in their desperation to keep their man-made system going, will put any warm body in any job, even if they aren't qualified. That's just begging for a disaster. The better answer is to reorganize, regroup, and pull together to work with what you have. It's not written in stone to have twelve teachers to teach all twelve grades of Sunday School! It may be that you need to form the group into larger classes and combine forces, so that you can have a few good teachers instead of a lot of bad ones. In other words, use what God has given you.

- **Emotion** – Napoleon said this about emotions: "The foremost quality of a commander is to keep a cool head, to receive accurate impressions of what is happening, and never fret or be amazed or be intoxicated by good news or bad." In other words, never succumb to your emotions.

  You will have emotions, but don't let them lead you or form your decisions. That is always fatal. Fear, for example, will cause a leader with an otherwise winning position to give up like a coward for no reason. Pride ruins the spirit of the church. It's a precursor to a fall, because it blinds us to our weaknesses and inclines us away from God's grace. Love, for as good a medicine as it is for many ills, is not the solution for dealing with wolves. Our emotions cloud our judgment, they consult the feelings instead of the truth, and they cause us to react to things instead of directing things. Joshua, when facing his task of invading the Promised Land, was counseled not to heed his fears.

> Have I not commanded you? Be strong and courageous. Do not be terrified; do not be discouraged, for the LORD your God will be with you wherever you go. (Joshua 1:9)

And when the rest of the church flames up in emotions, it's all the more important that you don't. Someone has to keep a cool head in the crisis. It also calms their fears, when they see the leader apparently in control of himself and the situation.

- **Casualties** – Remember that this is war, and there will be casualties. At first, Christians may think this is all a game, this training and dressing in uniforms and practice. But when their friends are lying on the field of battle bleeding and in pain, the reality of how serious this business is will begin to sink in.

  The enemy wants to hurt and destroy us. He's very adept at making people miserable and frustrated, sick and injured, bankrupt and lonely. But it's like that in every war; the fun wears off pretty quickly, and life becomes a grueling struggle to survive. The key is to come to grips with this reality and be ready for it.

  Casualties have to be taken care of. You should never leave the wounded to suffer on their own. The church has means of healing their diseases and injuries, and you will have special people in the church gifted to address those injuries. Besides, these people showed their willingness to fight and their loyalty to the cause, and you owe it to them to bring them back to health and full strength.

Just be sure not to stop the army over its casualties, however. The sight of blood – or of defeat, or failure, or sickness, or whatever happens to people in the vicissitudes of war – will tend to scare the rest of the members.

> Amasa lay wallowing in his blood in the middle of the road, and the man saw that all the troops came to a halt there. When he realized that everyone who came up to Amasa stopped, he dragged him from the road into a field and threw a garment over him. After Amasa had been removed from the road, all the men went on with Joab to pursue Sheba son of Bicri. (2 Samuel 20:12-13)

The war, however, must go on; we can't stop fighting because a few people go down around us. Take the wounded away quickly and take care of them, but keep everyone else moving.

Offense

Now we come to the very core of the idea of war, what most often comes to mind when people think of war: the fight itself.

As far as specific tactics, you can get all sorts of ideas from reading military manuals. What we want to focus on here are the basics as they apply to spiritual warfare. In our fight against our enemies, we need to learn two things: 1) what we have to achieve, and 2) the best way to achieve it.

The reason we have to fight in the first place is because our enemy hates us and is not going to listen to reason; he is trying to hurt or destroy us spiritually, to keep us from achieving our Mission. We therefore have to take more forceful measures. Our goal, then, is to *use such force against him that he backs away and leaves us alone*. Of course we have to decide which kind of war to fight – there are two kinds: a limited engagement where we are after a simple peace, or an unlimited war in which we are out to totally destroy our enemy. Depending on which we are after, we will use appropriate tactics to achieve that end.

So, we must apply force to throw the enemy back. It's time for offense; that's the whole point of going to war. We have to have a clear view of the enemy, and establish the right strategy and tactical skills to destroy him. Remember the three enemies that we have (the **world** and its temptations to sin, our **flesh** that in weakness falls prey to those temptations, and the **devil** who lies to us about the whole business of God and ourselves and the world we live in) – and then use the weapons that will most effectively defeat these enemies.

- *The world* – since the world's main appeal is a re-make of God's original creation, something that caters to our idea of the "perfect life" (materialism, power, and sensual pleasures), our strategy is twofold. *First*, we have to show the emptiness of the appeal; *second*, we have to replace it with a better option.

  It's going to be difficult to prove to people that this world isn't worth living for. Particularly in modern America, we are surrounded with stuff to the degree that we hardly get time away from dealing with our money and possessions. Our whole lives are taken up with them. Instead of fulfilling the deep needs of the soul, these empty promises appeal to our lusts, inflame our passions, deaden us toward the things of God, and leave us as burned out cinders fit only to be thrown away.

  We can show, if we take the time to look at it, that this world's stuff doesn't do what it's advertised to do. It particularly doesn't solve the real problems of life: like a drug, it desensitizes our souls so that we don't think about our problems. We float in a temporary euphoria enjoying our toys and things, but the problems still haven't gone away. In fact, those real problems of life have a way of roaring back upon us in the middle of our materialistic bliss unannounced.

> The ground of a certain rich man produced a good crop. He thought to himself, 'What shall I do? I have no place to store my crops.' Then he said, 'This is what I'll do. I will tear down my barns and build bigger ones, and there I will store all my grain and my goods. And I'll say to myself, "You have plenty of good things laid up for many years. Take life easy; eat, drink and be merry." But God said to him, 'You fool! This very night your life will be demanded from you. Then who will get what you have prepared for yourself?' (Luke 12:16-20)

God makes demands of us that no amount of sensual pleasures can answer. The rich man, remember, had everything he wanted in life, and ended up in Hell anyway. Lazarus, who didn't have a thing, evidently was rich in Heavenly treasures.

On the second point, our goal as Christians is the next world, not this one. The only way that God's world will become more real to us is if we deliberately focus on it: in prayer, in Bible study, in discussions with each other, in time spent "storing up treasures in Heaven."

> Since, then, you have been raised with Christ, set your hearts on things above, where Christ is seated at the right hand of God. Set your minds on things above, not on earthly things. For you died, and your life is now hidden with Christ in God. When Christ, who is your life, appears, then you also will appear with him in glory. (Colossians 3:1-4)

The key here is to use the things that show the emptiness of the world, and the value of God's world – the Word of God, as the Spirit opens it up to us. Both weapons are necessary in this battle. Once we have achieved a right view of both, we can then resist the temptations of the world, thank God for what he provides us daily, use our possessions to help others, long for spiritual treasures – all the right actions that a Christian left in this world should be doing.

- ***The flesh*** – This does not refer simply to our mortal bodies. There's something in us that loves to lust, that jumps at the chance to experience pleasure or show off in pride or rule over others. Paul calls it the "sinful nature," that aspect of our lives that drives us into rebellion against God's clear commands to the contrary.

We see it first in Eve's response to the temptation in the Garden. The fruit of the knowledge of good and evil appealed to her lusts – it was "good for food and pleasing to the eye, and also desirable for gaining wisdom" – so she ignored God's command about it and she took it. In other words, she consulted her own self and its desires instead of going by God's Word.

Since God's Word always results in life, rebellion against his Word is certain to bring death. *Listening to one's passions, contrary to God's command, is like pointing a gun at your head.* The life of immorality will destroy you in the end; it's as fatal a process as anything that can happen on a battlefield.

Let's continue to quote from that passage in Colossians, since Paul gives us the next weapon that will best kill the desire in us to long after this world.

> Put to death, therefore, whatever belongs to your earthly nature: sexual immorality, impurity, lust, evil desires and greed, which is idolatry. Because of these, the wrath of God is coming. You used to walk in these ways, in the life you once lived. But now you must rid yourselves of all such things as these: anger, rage, malice, slander, and filthy language from your lips. Do not lie to each other, since you have taken off your old self with its practices

and have put on the new self, which is being renewed in knowledge in the image of its Creator. (Colossians 3:5-10)

So, Jesus took on our flesh so that he could put to death our sinful nature and its illicit desires for this world.

The key to the Christian life is, of course, to become one with this crucified and resurrected man. The Spirit of Christ lives in us and makes that union a reality: he crucifies our flesh, and enables us to follow Jesus (carrying our cross) out of this world and into the next.

> For what the Law was powerless to do in that it was weakened by the sinful nature, God did by sending his own Son in the likeness of sinful man to be a sin offering. And so he condemned sin in sinful man, in order that the righteous requirements of the Law might be fully met in us, who do not live according to the sinful nature but according to the Spirit. (Romans 8:3-4)

We have now been delivered from the *power* of sin; it is no longer our master. Sanctification delivers us from the *presence* of sin – through the Spirit enabling us to walk with Christ, not after the desires of our flesh.

It's time to say "no" to the desires of your flesh.

> For the grace of God that brings salvation has appeared to all men. It teaches us to say "No" to ungodliness and worldly passions, and to live self-controlled, upright and godly lives in this present age, while we wait for the blessed hope—the glorious appearing of our great God and Savior, Jesus Christ, who gave himself for us to redeem us from all wickedness and to purify for himself a people that are his very own, eager to do what is good. (Titus 2:11-14)

The idea here then is to crucify the flesh. Deny yourself, take up your cross and follow him. Keep bringing your passions to the Cross of Christ and pleading with him to kill them in your heart, replacing them with the righteousness of Christ. Walk in the Spirit: i.e., listen to his counsel in the Word and go in the direction of Christ and Heaven, as he leads you. Don't live as the world lives, but live on a higher standard than they do. Confess your sins to others; that makes us think twice about living a hypocritical life! Live in humility, not pride, realizing that it's only the grace of God that keeps you walking in the straight and narrow path. Spend time with the saints, who are also struggling with sin, and encourage each other with the grace of Christ.

In other words, hit this problem about your sinful flesh hard, ruthlessly, persistently. Unless you take strong measures to defeat this enemy, you won't get anywhere as a Christian.

- *The devil* – Satan presents unique problems. First, he's a liar; you can count on it, that when you hear anything that contradicts God's Word, the devil is behind it. Second, he's a murderer. Through unjust, dirty warfare he destroys us. In fact, a clear mark of the devil's work in our world is wanton destruction, self-destruction, and senseless destruction.

  > You belong to your father, the devil, and you want to carry out your father's desire. He was a murderer from the beginning, not holding to the truth, for there is no truth in him. When he lies, he speaks his native language, for he is a liar and the father of lies. (John 8:44)

  The only antidote to the lies of the devil is the Word of God. For example, the devil would have us think that a little enjoyment of the world, a little indulgence of the flesh, and a casual attitude about God, isn't going to

War Principles

hurt anything. God's Word, however, shows us the utter falsehood of such a destructive point of view.

The Bible reveals the true and full glory of God, our complete obligation to the Creator, our helpless and alarming spiritual state as sinners in his Kingdom, the emptiness of this world and its pleasures, the only way to salvation in Christ, the reality of the spiritual war that we are in the middle of, the full rewards and pleasures of the next world, the true end of this world destined for destruction, and the truly evil and ruthless nature of our enemies. Knowledge, they say, is power, and knowing the truth of these matters puts us in a peculiar position now. It's not at all the way the devil explained things to us. We have been deceived about a great many things, and unless we take immediate and drastic action we will be as lost as he is.

> If you hold to my teaching, you are really my disciples. Then you will know the truth, and the truth will set you free. (John 8:31-32)

And that is why Jesus came – to "deliver us from evil," to "destroy the works of the devil," and to "set us free from sin and death." The Bible is literally our only guidebook out of this mess.

So, church work is literally based on teaching the Word of God. When people resist learning the Bible, they are resisting the medicine. Don't allow that. Teach, instruct, train, drill in the principles of the Word until everyone has it mastered and memorized. You can't do too much in this area. Our minds were made for learning and investigation; and there's nothing better in this world to learn and fill our minds with than the truth from God.

As we focus on the Word like this, life starts straightening out. By the power of the Word, and the Spirit who reveals it to us, the destructive work of the devil will slowly be reversed in our lives and we can start breathing freely in the atmosphere of God's liberating spiritual world.

Remember too that these enemies work not just on an individual level, but at the church level also. The kinds of temptations and wealth and power and misinformation that hinder the work of the church would necessarily be different from the kinds that appeal to an individual. We should be familiar with both spheres of operations.

Offensive weapons

The Church has weapons that will destroy these three enemies of ours. It's a ridiculous mistake for us to resort to the world's weapons. As Paul told us, our enemies simply can't stand before the awesome firepower of what we Christians have available to us.

> For though we live in the world, we do not wage war as the world does. The weapons we fight with are not the weapons of the world. On the contrary, they have divine power to demolish strongholds. We demolish arguments and every pretension that sets itself up against the knowledge of God, and we take captive every thought to make it obedient to Christ. (2 Corinthians 10:3-5)

The question is, do we have the necessary skill to use these weapons in the context of the Church's Mission? Let's look at some examples of using spiritual weapons.

- **Prayer** – Instead of the usual "Lord, please heal Aunt Matilda's toe" kinds of prayers, focus on the treasures of Heaven and the Kingdom of Christ. Jesus did tell us, did he not, to pray like that?

    > So do not worry, saying, 'What shall we eat?' or 'What shall we drink?' or 'What shall we wear?' For the pagans run after all these things, and your Heavenly Father knows that you need them. But seek first his kingdom and his

righteousness, and all these things will be given to you as well. (Matthew 6:31-33)

People are so obsessed with praying for material things and comforts that they forget about the great Mission at hand. The Mission is never absent from Christ's mind; he likes to hear it from us also, on a daily basis, since we are part of his army charged with helping build his Kingdom.

Prayer is like calling down firepower on the enemy's position. God has special answers for our specific problems, and all we have to do is ask for them. We know where the problem is, and we know that only God can solve this particular problem – in his way.

Prayer is also a matter of bowing down before the King and finding out what he wants us to do. So many people think that we are telling God something in prayer, when actually he already knows about the whole situation. What he wants is for us to be quiet for once and listen: these things (as he described them in his Word) are what you need here. Successful prayer happens when you find out the truth about God and what he intends to do.

For myself, I've divided up the great issues of Christ's Kingdom across the week, as David taught us with his agenda. On Mondays I pray about the Heavenly Jerusalem, the spiritual Kingdom that Jesus is setting up for us – that the church would seize that idea and focus on spiritual treasures instead of this world. On Tuesdays I pray about our spiritual enemies and plead with God to go out with our armies against them. And so on through the rest of the week. On the weekend I pray about the two aspects of the Mission itself. This kind of prayer focuses on what matters most to God's people. These things are, after all, what God wants for us!

- **Bible study** – The Bible has to become a textbook for God's people, not just a promise book. It requires study, and only through study will we grasp its lessons. Back up everything – *everything* – that happens in the Church and in your life with the Bible's teachings.

    We have to keep in mind what the purpose of the Bible is: it's the revelation of God. So focus on God himself in every story that you study. Study his ways, his works, his names, his likes and dislikes, his commands, his Kingdom, his many roles in his dealings with men (like Redeemer, Judge, Creator, King, etc.). Such a concentration on God will keep Bible study free of a man-centered – and therefore empty and powerless – religion that does nobody any good. Then pray for what you learned about.

    And remember too what the purpose of the Old Testament is – that it describes Christ, the Son of the Father, and our relationship to God through him. It makes clear what we need as God's people, what we are, where we are, how to get clear of the world, how to avoid and fight the enemy. The New Testament steps further into the mystery and describes the New Man and how we become one with him. In order to master these concepts, you will have to study the Bible very seriously for a long time. And once you have mastered them, you can start using the Bible to successfully solve many problems in your life.

- **Fellowship** – Fellowship is a powerful weapon for keeping unity of purpose, correction, discipline and training, encouragement, and vision among the ranks of Christians. So instead of wasting a golden opportunity by focusing on sports or politics, start using the spiritual gifts on each other. "Psalms, hymns, and spiritual songs," encouragement, reconciliation, help, enlighten-ment – anything that will bring the Body itself together and make it stronger spiritually.

Other aspects of our fellowship with each other depend on the fruit of the Spirit, and the gifts of the Spirit. The fruit (Galatians 5:22-23) corrects our nasty nature, and makes it possible for us to work together and work with God. The gifts of the Spirit put people in touch with God, and stimulate faith and spiritual growth. So anything we can do to nurture these two aspects of the Spirit among the group will go a long way to destroying the work of the enemy and building Christ's Kingdom.

Keep in mind that only a well-trained group will be able to do these things! You may be leafing through this book right now and thinking that you'd like to start right here. It won't work. If you try to drop people into deep waters before they can swim, they will either leave you or drown in the attempt. You have to go back to that methodical and rigorous training described earlier in this book before you can expect your church members to operate on this mature level.

Tactics

Tactics involves the battlefield itself: what is the best way to go about fighting the enemy? In contrast with strategy (which focuses on the wider picture and maneuvers of war), tactics involves maneuvers against the enemy and how we actually apply firepower against him.[12]

As for offensive tactics, we should focus on four all-important points.

- **Full combat power** – Wait for the right moment to strike, and then strike with all the force that you have. Don't hold anything back. Overwhelm the enemy with enough force to drive him back and destroy his position. The idea is to pour on so much firepower that it surprises and overwhelms him; his front line simply

---

[12] General Halleck defined *strategy* as those aspects of war beyond the range of a cannon shot, and *tactics* being whatever we do within the range of a cannon shot.

can't stand up to all the destruction that you are raining down on him. A half-effort never won a battle.

- **Seize and maintain the initiative** – Don't let the enemy dictate the battle; *you* drive *him* around the battlefield. Move first, pull him into dangerous places, hit him by surprise, make a fake move in one direction (called a *feint*) and then hit him in another spot where he isn't looking. Don't stop moving, and don't let him rest. You should never have to react to his actions; you should make him have to react to you. That's keeping the initiative: you are in control of how the battle flows, not him. Then when he is exhausted and has had enough he will retreat. Then follow him!

- **Hit the weakest point** – Don't aim at the enemy's strongest point but at his weakest. He has spent a lot of time building up his ranks in his own way; so he will be weakest in other areas where he isn't expecting an attack. His flanks – the sides, where his forces are thinned out – are the ideal areas to strike. From there you can roll up his line, one by one, and make the whole thing collapse. Watch to see if he moves his forces and then hit him at the point from where he pulled them away; take advantage of him thinning his line out like this.

- **Divide and conquer** – Don't take on his entire army. Somehow get it to split up, get separated – then you can take on smaller pieces with your entire force. Once you have dealt with that small piece with your whole force, turn to the next one.

Give a lot of thought to these tactics and study how you would apply them to spiritual warfare. For example, during Bible study, don't just hunker down on a single verse and ask everyone how they feel about it. If you are talking about salvation, study the whole scope of the subject throughout the Bible. Go back to Creation and find out the true basis of how the New Creation works. Study the deliverance from Egypt in depth. Study the wars of David in depth. Learn the depths of the Law, the sin that stains our hearts, and the utter holiness of the sacrifices that cleanse that sin. Listen to the Prophets as they probe the human heart and uncover hidden aspects of sin. Do justice to the idea of salvation in your teaching and give the church members some real meat in their own struggle against sin. This is what I mean about hitting the enemy with all that you have – people will no longer have any misconceptions about what salvation really is!

When you pray, hit hard at the weakest point of the enemy's lines. Don't just pray for general "blessings," but pray for the salvation of particular sinners. If someone comes to you with a crisis, home in on the real problem and, through prayer, shake that person loose from the grip of the enemy; aim at the sins that he or she is struggling under. If he will see his sin, and turn to Christ to free him and forgive him, you have just broken the link that held him in bondage – and you can now take this person a long way into the Kingdom.

When you have a group of troublemakers, isolate the ringleader and confront him directly about the damage he is doing to the church. Divide and conquer; don't take on the whole group. Put the pressure on that one person until he changes or leaves. When you do this to him, everyone else starts identifying him as a target and will stay away from him for fear of getting dragged down with him. Group psychology kicks in here: people will usually back away from a person who is in trouble. That's why Jesus said to treat him as you would a tax collector.

> But now I am writing you that you must not associate with anyone who calls himself a brother but is sexually immoral or greedy, an idolater or a slanderer, a drunkard or a swindler. With such a man do not even eat. (1 Corinthians 5:11)

Defense

Offensive warfare is by far the most costly in terms of supplies and energy. After a while we start running out of both. You simply can't maintain that high level of activity forever. At some point (hopefully after giving the enemy a really bad time!) you will have to slow down, and then think about digging in. If you are not open to this, you *will* learn the hard way: your troops will get weary, slow down, and then suddenly find themselves having to fend off the enemy coming back at them with *its* full force in retaliation. A good leader will be ready for this.

Defense means backing up to a safe place to get replenished, rested, and reorganized to go back to the fight. Defense is never a permanent feature of a winning army. It's necessary, but it's only a temporary situation. Armies have never won wars sitting in their fortresses. Clausewitz, the great military theoretician of the nineteenth century, taught that defense is not just a shield, but "a shield made up of well-directed blows." In other words, you may need the safety of a fortress, but don't stop responding to the enemy in your safety. Keep directing cannon fire at him from the walls. The idea is to get some breathing time so that you can come back out fighting.

Defense takes less energy and resources; it's much more efficient and less costly than the offense. So take advantage of that.

- **Reform quickly** – Battles are costly affairs, and you will find, when you get time to look over the situation in your retreat, that there is a lot of damage control to do. Use this time of relative peace to reform and resupply. You will probably have to encourage the troops again, since what they just went through was a traumatic thing; they will need their nerves and courage strengthened to go back out to the fight.

- **Maintain standards** – Never change your high standards during the defensive stage. It's criminal how the church has given away its standards of truth during the twentieth century, just when we needed a fixed point in morals and truth in an age where everything became relative and changeable. Our God never changes, his Law never changes, and the way to Heaven never changes. There is no reason for you to change the truth in any way in a changing culture (usually done with the excuse that it has be "more relevant"). Fighting the enemy is draining and painful, and the temptation during a rest period is to let down on the standards and quit being such a strict Christian. But that's like tearing the wall of the fortress down and letting in the enemy. You simply cannot let up on strict discipline, no matter how tired you are.

> Anyone who breaks one of the least of these commandments and teaches others to do the same will be called least in the kingdom of Heaven, but whoever practices and teaches these commands will be called great in the kingdom of Heaven. For I tell you that unless your righteousness surpasses that of the Pharisees and the teachers of the Law, you will certainly not enter the kingdom of Heaven. (Matthew 5:19-20)

- **Watch for an opening** – Take time to retreat to a safe place when you need to, but don't be satisfied to stay there. If you are always on the defensive, there will never be an end to the battle. It will go on and on. You have to move out eventually and put an end to your enemy. But since defense takes less energy, devote your attention to watching your enemy. Wait for that moment when he makes a mistake, or gets tired, or spreads his forces too thin. He has to eventually. Be busy getting your forces ready for that moment – resupplied, gathered in force again, and eager to finish the fight. When that door of opportunity opens (you may only get one chance at it) go after it with all that you have.

Defensive work in the church involves two main areas: *first*, a team protecting the rest of the church while it rests and re-trains and refits. *Second*, the whole group needs to focus on healing its wounds, learning from its recent experiences, refitting for future battles, drills and training to keep in shape, and planning new strategies and tactics. It should be a busy and productive time for the church.

Movement

The Marines pride themselves on their speed and mobility. They are a fighting force that bases its tactics on movement, not stagnation. Probably the single biggest lesson learned during World War I was that trench warfare doesn't work.

Too many churches aren't making any progress at all. They aren't designed to make progress. Nobody is targeting the problem, nobody is even willing to admit to a problem. There's no measure of growth or change, nor is anybody interested in measuring them. Church is just a gathering where a few nice platitudes are said from the pulpit, some general encouragement is given, and people go back home. No testing, no changes, no reports on spiritual movement, no spiritual growth. It's about as aimless and without purpose as a group can be without actually disbanding from lack of interest.

It's time for the leaders of the church to put things in motion. The church is in a lot of danger that it has to get away from *now*. A lot of changes must be started to move the church from its position of weakness and ignorance so that it becomes a fighting force. The church has to move to better ground to fight from. The enemy is always moving, and the church has to hit him head-on.

You, as the leader, have to make sure that real progress is made in the following areas.

- **Spiritual growth** – Let's make sure at the beginning that we are aiming at the real thing. Even with all this emphasis on military procedure, we mustn't lose sight of the fact that we aren't simply out to make an army. That's the means to the end, but it's not the end in itself. The goal is to become like Christ, to shed our sins, to become Heavenly-minded and love God. Though this military training is necessary, it's like a uniform that we have to wear for the job at hand. Someday we are going to shed this uniform and "study war no more." We have to be soldiers because we have

War Principles

this unavoidable problem right now of enemies trying to get in the way of our spiritual goal. It's an added responsibility, and we should get good at it; but it's no more than an unfortunate element in life that complicates the real issue at hand. So the thing we are measuring is our spiritual stature, our spiritual maturity, our wisdom, our spiritual-mindedness, our holiness, our walk with God. And a fighting spirit makes that possible.

- **Quick response** – Movement means you can move and move quickly. Several things factor into this issue: *first*, is your group (and you!) on a state of alert so that you move out quickly to attack problems? Or are you partying, asleep, and generally unaware that there are battles going on?

  > Then he returned to his disciples and found them sleeping. "Simon," he said to Peter, "are you asleep? Could you not keep watch for one hour? Watch and pray so that you will not fall into temptation. The spirit is willing, but the body is weak." (Mark 14:37-38)

  Second, are you organized to be on the road in a short time? Even if they are caught asleep, a well-trained and organized team can be dressed, equipped, and headed off to battle in a matter of minutes. The issue here is that you don't want to waste time addressing problems, because problems (and the people who cause them) are usually moving very quickly to catch you off guard. As General Forrest once (reputedly) said, to win a battle you have to "git thar fustest with the mostest."

- **Following the terrain** – Remember that the lay of the land determines your tactics. You can't tackle a mountain, or cross a deep river, and expect to have an easy time of things. Follow the valleys, cut through gorges, and don't plunge into deep forests.

What this looks like in the church setting is this: Don't go around the parents to reach the kids, or around the husband to reach the wife. If you do, you will encounter fierce resistance. I saw a wife burst into tears once during a Bible study and, in front of the whole group, complain about what she didn't like about her husband. The pastor, who was leading the study, stopped everything and took her side, to the point of gathering a group of other women around her knees to encourage her as she sat there sobbing. The husband, who was also sitting there in the group, was mortified and humiliated, and understandably furious for being made a fool of in public. Both the wife and the pastor inexcusably went around him in sheer disrespect. The two ended up getting a divorce. So much for the pastor's skill at handling a crisis.

In other words, don't try to change reality;[13] work *with* it and make it work for you. Here the pastor should have asked the husband to take his wife out of the meeting, and then met with them later in counseling.

- **Checklist** – While in training, we have the leisure and opportunity to put all our resources together and make things work. It works well, and we can see why – when there's no pressure on us to divert our attention. Just don't forget that all those strengths are going to be needed out in the field of battle as well.

In our haste to go to battle, we may forget to take something along, or tend to think that we can do without it. But we can no more do without it than when we were in training. You will have to stop and give your troops a rest; you will have to make sure they have food and supplies; you will have to transport them where they are needed. The training should have made the point: we learned about *all* that we will need for the

---

[13] That is, God-ordained reality. There is such a thing as praying to remove obstacles that ought not to be there! See Mark 11:23.

fight. Don't leave out any essential item, or you will find out the hard way that "for the lack of a nail, the war was lost." In other words, you will have to carry the entire support system with you when you go out to battle. Make a checklist so that you don't forget anything.

- **Secrecy** – One thing that you don't want to do is broadcast all of your movements to the enemy! For some strange reason, "conscientious Christians" feel that they have to tell even their enemies everything on their heart, and everything they are doing – for the sake of honesty and truthfulness.

The military knows better than to publish their battle plans for the enemy's perusal. They have whole departments assigned to the tasks of deception, secrecy, misinformation, and counter-intelligence. We also have abundant scriptural warrant for not being so stupid in dealing with the enemy: Rahab is listed in the roll-call of faithful saints for misleading the pagans of Jericho (Hebrews 11:31); God himself lured the Egyptians into a trap (Exodus 14); David's counselor Hushai led Absalom off in the wrong direction and so helped save the kingdom (2 Samuel 16).

Don't misunderstand me: I'm not proposing that we turn to lying to achieve our ends. That's the enemy's strategy. But you don't have to publish everything either; there's such a thing as handing over to the enemy what they need to destroy you. I know of an associate pastor who was so ambitious for power that he was trying to get as many of the departments in the church under his authority that he could. One of the other pastors decided that he would simply go to this man and pour his heart out to him, and reason with him, and "love him," in an effort to get him to back off from his power plays. I'm afraid he didn't know his man. This tactic backfired; the first pastor saw an opportunity to browbeat him too, to dominate him, and eventually swallow up his department as well. Chamberlain, remember, tried the same thing with Hitler in the months before World War II erupted, and unwittingly gave Hitler exactly what he wanted. The ruthless Hitler knew exactly how to manipulate the naïve British Prime Minister and send him back home with empty promises and a war that nobody could stop.

On the other hand, Stonewall Jackson almost never told anybody what he was planning on doing. His theory was that even the best-intentioned subordinates would probably leak the information too early, ruining his plans.

The point is this: keep your own counsel when you can smell the work of the enemy. Make your plans, and then suddenly, unexpectedly, bring out your army and your solution to attack the problem. Surprise almost always throws back the enemy in confusion.

- **Lines of operation** – We have mentioned already how important it is to keep our lines of operation open. This is our lifeline back to God, to our spiritual supplies, to our retreat into the Fortress. But when you are on the march, and particularly when you are in battle, keeping that lifeline open and accessible is one of the hardest things you have to do. As you get deeper into enemy territory, the enemy is always threatening to cut it off by a surprise attack. You have to assign more security to protect it or you will get cut off from your only safety and supply.

  One effective way to protect those lines is to assign the duty to a team. Put them in charge of bringing the church members back to God through prayer, fellowship and Bible study. Keep them busy checking on the spiritual welfare of all the members, and they can report dangerous situations to you that you can then deal with. Make sure all members keep praying and studying the Bible in the middle of their responsibilities. The basics are still important!

- **Unified responses** – The reason we trained *together* back in camp is so that we can fight *together* in battle. The victory is not won by one person, but by many. And it's particularly effective when the whole group acts at the same time, doing the same thing – to apply maximum firepower to the enemy's line. Of all times to do what you are told, the time of battle is the most important. It is crucial that everyone be agreed and everyone do their part, without hesitation, according to the rules, energetically and willingly. Under fire, a lot of people have many reasons for wanting to back out and quit. That's why the military has come up with some effective methods for keeping people in line, doing their job, when the time comes. Now is not the time to succumb to fear or rebellion.

I've seen churches who were damaged by the work of troublemakers (they show up from time to time) and the responses in the church ranged from "loving the sinner" to wanting to shoot him on sight. Almost everyone had an opinion on what to do, and almost no two people thought alike on the subject. The result was that the church – and particularly its leadership – had no way of dealing with the trouble. Nothing could be done with them because there was no majority decision on it. That, of course, is the perfect setup for the troublemakers; they can do the most damage in an atmosphere of indecision and confusion. We do have procedures in the Bible for dealing with every kind of problem. We have to follow through on them – *all* of us. If the church is instructed to see someone out the door ("treat them as you would a publican or sinner" – Matthew 18:17) then *everyone* has to treat him like that, or the discipline won't work at all. It is particularly frustrating to leadership when the church won't back them up on what they know is the right thing to do. If this is the way the church fights its battles, then they will never win.

- **Traveling light** – The war of maneuver requires that you don't burden your troops with more than they need. In the church, that translates into doing only what God told you to do and leave the rest to the Lord to handle. It's instructive that Jesus has the same attitude:

> For my yoke is easy and my burden is light. (Matthew 11:30)

The Early Church knew that the old Jewish system of the "heavy load" of the Law, or what they turned the Law into, was a burden that Christians need not carry. It gets in the way of their life of faith.

> It seemed good to the Holy Spirit and to us not to burden you with anything beyond the following requirements. (Acts 15:28)

Paul knew that people have a tendency to multiply rules and regulations to make themselves appear more "holy," when really such rules don't accomplish at all what they claim.

> Since you died with Christ to the basic principles of this world, why, as though you still belonged to it, do you submit to its rules: "Do not handle! Do not taste! Do not touch!"? These are all destined to perish with use, because they are based on human commands and teachings. Such regulations indeed have an appearance of wisdom, with their self-imposed worship, their false humility and their harsh treatment of the body, but they lack any value in restraining sensual indulgence. (Colossians 2:20-23)

The Christian life is actually very simple; follow the great leaders of the past as they show you what you really need in your walk of faith. They have a way of simplifying the requirements.

> Watch out for those dogs, those men who do evil, those mutilators of the flesh. For it is *we* who are the circumcision, we who *worship by the Spirit of God*, who *glory in Christ Jesus*, and who *put no confidence in the flesh*. (Philippians 3:1)

There's another way that modern Christians burden themselves unnecessarily: they build huge megachurches costing millions of dollars, and then they have to spend the majority of their time scheming how to pay for such monstrosities. That time would be better spent on spiritual training instead of bake sales, basketball teams, book clubs, cheerleading training, and other gimmicks that churches think up to try to get "tithing" members to join the church and pay the bills.

- **Follow the waypoints** – During the strategy sessions, the commanders study their maps intensely and form detailed plans for the entire operation. An essential part of those plans are the *waypoints* – those places on the map that the army will arrive at, at specific times, on the way to the battlefield.

  These waypoints are crucial. They are places of safety and security and secrecy. They are places of supply, where needed depots will be waiting. They are places of coordination where different elements will meet at the right time to coordinate their efforts for the coming battle. If you want your church to succeed, plan on using these critical waypoints. By God's design they serve as supply and security and coordination points for the people of God. They are signs that you are going in the right direction.

  The Bible itself is the guide for the fighting church. It shows us the points of spiritual maturity that we have to attain, it shows us where God is and where not to go, it shows us the characteristics of true Christianity, it shows us marks of readiness for battle against spiritual enemies. So insist that Christianity is the business of becoming holy, of crucifying sin, of turning from the world, of making new friendships with other believers – in other words, it's not being like everyone else in the world. As you struggle against a culture full of confusing and immoral standards, pull the Bible out for the church to use as the standard. These are what we have to attain to; these are the points that you have to pass on your way to Heaven. God specially designed the truths in the Bible to be our waypoints of life.

> So that you may become blameless and pure, children of God without fault in a crooked and depraved generation, in which you shine like stars in the universe as you hold out the word of life—in order that I may boast on the day of Christ that I did not run or labor for nothing. (Philippians 2:15-16)

Esprit

Esprit is important to keep the motivation up. People have to believe in the cause, so much so that they are willing to change their schedules, do without things they ordinarily enjoy, spend time training and preparing, and go to battle with grim determination to win. They are willing to give their lives for the cause.

It takes a special kind of leader to develop *esprit*. Most leaders are not very good at helping the group develop this spirit, or they simply expect everyone to be motivated on their own. But good leaders realize that the average member is full of fears, ignorance, hesitation, over-confidence – all sorts of emotions that actually hinder proper motivation and fighting spirit. And when the *esprit* is gone, the problems loom larger, tempers get short, complaining increases, friction develops between departments – the group starts splitting into factions and individuals instead of remaining united.

So the good leader helps develop *esprit*. He shows the group the progress they have made. He helps them see the damage that the enemy is still out there doing, and what they can do to stop him. He brings in testimony from those who have been successfully fighting the battle. He finds out what the group is missing, or what their battle wounds are, and sees to their needs.

One way to restore fighting spirit is to pull some battle-weary troops back from the front line and give them a different assignment for a while. The long days (or weeks or years!) of fighting the same battle wears a person down tremendously. Just a change of scenery, a change of responsibility, lifts the spirits again.

Alliances

In peacetime every nation tends to its own affairs. But in war, it's a fool of a commander who ignores the benefits of getting allies to help in the effort. People may not have gotten along well in the past, but when a danger arises that threatens everyone's security, it's wise to put our differences aside and work together to defeat the enemy.

Ever since the Reformation the Protestant churches have shown nothing but a divisive spirit. That's so foolish: we have the truth, the resources, the clear way to Heaven – but like bickering children we can't seem to cooperate and take advantage of these rich treasures. The Roman Catholic church still shames us in its ability to keep its unity. On our side, not only do warring denominations multiply worldwide, but even two churches on the same street won't work together despite how close as they are theologically as Protestants.

In the meantime our enemies are having a field day because of our in-house strife. The church has no unified response to the problems of our society. You will find even the church supporting the programs of immorality and godlessness of our decadent culture. Liberal Theology has led the rebellion against the Bible itself, so that it's a rare Bible school or seminary that isn't infected to some degree with its anti-Bible poison. Multiply each of those schools by thousands, and you will begin to grasp the influence that the enemy has had on our nation's churches who receive these "trained professionals" who don't know what they are doing spiritually. Today's church has no unified statement of the truth, or of the Mission.

We can't win when we are so splintered and divided. But then I suppose Christians aren't going to get along until all of us are threatened with destruction. It's when the war actually starts, and we start dying by the thousands, that we will finally wake up (hopefully!) and take decisive action. When that happens, people get real about what's really important; they quit playing games and get down to the business at hand.

Personally I believe that any two churches can get along if they both believe in the Apostles' Creed. It has the minimum standards for the Christian faith; anything else we might hold to is a secondary matter compared to these primary truths. Perhaps that's not enough; perhaps we need something more to unify us – but at least I'm looking for what will pull us together because I see the war coming that will force us to work together. I have no respect for any Christian, church member or leader, who refuses to consider such a possibility and won't work toward that end. Some may think that I'm being unrealistic and naïve, but in light of the commands of Scripture I have to believe that such a thing is not only possible, it is mandatory.

> I have given them the glory that you gave me, that they may be one as we are one: I in them and you in me. May they be brought to complete unity to let the world know that you sent me and have loved them even as you have loved me. (John 17:22-23)

> Make every effort to keep the unity of the Spirit through the bond of peace. There is one body and one Spirit – just as you were called to one hope when you were called – one Lord, one faith, one baptism; one God and Father of all, who is over all and through all and in all. (Ephesians 4:3-6)

But then I'm a military theorist; when it comes to solving problems, I tend toward the practical. You have to unify if you want to defeat the enemy. The oft-quoted maxim of "divide and conquer" is true in this case: the enemy has successfully divided us, and now we have no power.

It's our duty, and it's practical common sense, to get along with other Christians. We have to pool our resources: instead of dividing over what makes us unique and different from other churches, we ought to be utilizing those differences for maximum effect. For example, though I can't bring myself to baptize an infant (I simply don't see my way clear to do that), I told my first church that if anybody there wanted their infants baptized, I would call on a Presbyterian minister friend and ask him to come do it for them. I was determined to keep secondary matters in the background and focus on primary matters instead.

It makes no sense to me for Christians who share the same Mission – salvation from sin through Christ, and the hope of Heaven – to stop at the door of the Temple and shoot at each other. Such stupidity is costing us this war. We are doing exactly what the enemy wants us to do. On Judgment Day our Commander-in-Chief will take a hard line against his division commanders refusing to communicate, to help each other, or to coordinate their efforts against the enemy – in rebellion against his clear orders to cooperate.

The point: don't make your commander angry!

Problems within

You would think that the enemy is enough trouble to handle during a battle. Unfortunately you also have the enemy in your own ranks at the same time. Backstabbers, gossips, troublemakers, spies, legalists, schemers, self-serving and greedy opportunists – they gather around armies like vultures and add to your troubles. In my first church, I was shocked that Christians would act like that. Now I know that not everyone who calls themselves Christians *are* Christians; not everyone is on the same page. While the battle with the enemy rages, you also have to deal with the traitors and deserters and troublemakers within the ranks.

You will also have problems that aren't criminal but are nevertheless bothersome, things that shouldn't have happened – but they have a way of showing themselves at inopportune times. They are results of oversights, lack of training and lack of preparation. You just have to deal with them when they come up, and it's no use getting angry and frustrated. It's part of the reality of war: battles have a way of revealing your weaknesses that don't show up in peacetime. Keep alert, and be ready to meet any unexpected situation intelligently and faithfully.

- **Traitors & rebels** – Jesus *did* warn us that wolves would appear among us. Many of the problems in the church are simply troublesome and come under the heading of "sins to get saved from." But some things are unacceptable: they are the work of our enemy, designed to steer us away from the Mission itself. They must be dealt with quickly and decisively.

  Some people will "introduce destructive heresies" (2 Peter 2:1) into the group. Some troublemakers are "insubordinate" (1 Timothy 1:9) and rebel against the authority of the church, and try to spread their rebellion. Some tempt people to "follow other gods" (Deuteronomy 13:2) other than the God of the Bible and his published truth. I'm using actual Scriptural phrases here, to show you what the Bible calls such activities. In each case, the remedy is plain: confront them, isolate them, and destroy their influence. The military shoots people like these. We don't have firing squads in the church today, but we do have the obligation to shut these people down before they spread their poison among the whole group.

  The reason we have been told to use this summary remedy with these particular problems is twofold: *first*, it's actually our spiritual enemies working through these troublemakers. We have to strike hard against the real enemy and get rid of him. Neutralize and eliminate his tool, and he loses his influence among us. *Second*, you are probably going to get nowhere trying to talk to these people and reason with them; "loving them" (a common remedy tried by many a well-meaning but naïve leader) won't work. The answer is to separate them away from the group, and let Satan teach them the lesson they need to learn – you won't. (1 Corinthians 5:5)

- **Logistics** – For all the careful planning that we do in the church, a battle will inevitably uncover our weaknesses and lack of foresight. Supplies will not be where they need to be; helpers and teachers will get sick, retire, move, quit, or otherwise go off-line and put the church in a difficult situation. There's no way we can predict what will happen in times of stress and trouble, and obviously those times will reveal our limitations and shortcomings. So, you have to be ready for these circumstances and take decisive action to fill the gap.

  One practical problem in the church is that most people aren't going to make it to all of your training sessions. Inevitably, when a crisis comes up, your members will need the very lesson that they missed a month ago. There's no sense in beating them over the head; the task at hand is to bring them up to speed immediately and get them going again. Work overtime, assign a special team to the task, and do whatever you can to give them what they missed.

- **Movement** – In a well-trained unit, you can and should expect them to follow orders and move in unison. The combination of good training, strict obedience, and established procedures to solve specific problems is a winning formula – but all the parts of the system have to be in place for this to work. You should expect, however, that it won't always be this simple. People get confused, they react emotionally to problems, they forget the lessons, they misread your instructions and do the wrong thing at the worst time. Even in the most organized and spiritually mature church, occasionally you will have people going the wrong direction and doing the wrong things.

Whatever you do, don't stop the entire group just to correct the person or persons at fault. The issue at hand is the battle, and we must always be maintaining full energy and purpose against the enemy. While you maintain control and direction of the army, assign someone else to take care of the problem. It's probably just a matter of mis-information and confusion, and it won't take long to correct the problem. But you have to put someone on it right away, because it can cause confusion in the rest of the church if you don't.

- **Different levels of expertise** – In the military it's easier to assign a trained regiment, disciplined and ready for battle, to a specific task. The raw recruits are held back in training camp until they are ready. In the church, however, that's much more difficult to do. Individual members are unmercifully singled out by the enemy no matter what their level of expertise may be. Again, there's no sense blaming anybody for this difficult situation; you just have to deal with it. When a spiritually immature Christian is hit with problems that are too big for him to handle, then assign a more mature Christian to his case to help him along. That's why the older women are told to instruct the younger women, and the older men the younger – wisdom from experience can help train and lead the passions of youth to keep them out of trouble. (Titus 2) This is a group effort, not an army of one.

TRANSFER OF COMMAND

The time will come when you must pass on your responsibilities to others. The ideal is to have a peaceful, successful transfer – which can only come about as a result of careful planning ahead of time. You have to make sure the sheep will continue to be fed, and the programs will continue to run, in someone else's hands.

TRANSFER OF COMMAND

General de Gaulle, in response to someone's comment about how indispensible he was to the cause, said that the graveyards are filled with indispensible people. No matter how important we think we are to the cause, our time will come to move on. But then that fits in with our theology: Jesus alone is the King, the Rock, the Commander-in-Chief. He has all the resources for his army, and he lives forever. What would he need us for beyond our short time of service? He raises up new leaders for every generation.

You must keep this in mind while you are leading the church. They have to develop a dependence on Christ, not on you. They have to learn how to follow his orders and use his resources. Your job is to show them how to do that. There have been many stellar performers in the church who didn't develop that side of their ministry, with the result that, after they were gone, the ministry collapsed. Evidently much of what was going on was centered around the man instead of God. You are not helping people when you do that.

You have to prepare for the future, then, while you are working in the church. In fact, you need to start working on a smooth transfer of responsibilities from the first day. We have covered a lot of important principles so far in our study, but now look at them as concepts that will build security and long-range staying power into your group. They are not only beneficial for your present group, but also for the next generation. The ability to pass on the torch depends on the kind of foundation that you laid down years ago. You have to work with the future in mind as well as the present.

> Only be careful, and watch yourselves closely so that you do not forget the things your eyes have seen or let them slip from your heart as long as you live. Teach them to your children and to their children after them. (Deuteronomy 4:9)

Stability

One thing you don't want to do is pass on a church full of problems to the next person. For one thing, you will be telling him in big letters that you had no idea what you were doing in the ministry. He will blame you for all the trouble he has to go through straightening out problems that should never have been left to develop. Your reputation as a church leader will suffer as a result.

Stability and peace come from a well-laid foundation; they don't just happen on their own.

- **Self-feeding group** – Teach the church how to feed itself spiritually. As you know if you have ever had children, it's fun to feed the infants at first, and necessary because they can't do it themselves. But something is seriously wrong if they grow up and still can't feed themselves. Yet in today's churches, there are many "Christians" who don't know the beginning of the Bible from the end. They can't pray for themselves (they are always asking the pastor to pray for them – when they should be praying for him!). They can't see to their own souls; they have no idea what's wrong in their lives, and they can't fix their own problems. They don't have any idea of how to follow the Lord, let alone do anything useful in the church for other people. They become a drain on the entire church.

    I've seen the problem, and I've seen the reason for it: the pastors don't teach the people how to feed themselves. For some reason, the pastor wants to look like an expert and get all the glory for himself. So he delivers fine-sounding sermons and lessons that nobody understands or remembers from Sunday to Sunday. He doesn't teach people how to study the Bible for themselves; he keeps this information to himself as if it's a trade secret. He wants people to be completely dependent on him; maybe it makes him feel needed, and gives him job security. The result is that nobody can do anything on their own; they need their pastor to be a "priest" for them for even the simplest things.

Not only is a church like that a spiritual disaster, it will have no life after the pastor is gone. Your goal is to get these people to stand on their own two feet, spiritually. You must be a trainer, not a showman. Teach them how to study, to pray, to witness, to walk with God, to resist the world – just as you would teach your own children the skills of life so that they won't be helpless when they graduate and go out into the world on their own. *That* builds a stable church of mature, responsible Christians.

- **Good communications** – We have said a good bit so far about the importance of communications, but it figures into the stability of the church as well. Insecurity, potentially fatal problems, wrong solutions applied to poorly understood problems, fear, misunderstanding and distrust among the members – all this and more will demoralize and destroy a group over time, not give it stability. Good communications keep these kinds of things from happening in the first place. In other words, make sure everyone is talking to each other, and being honest with each other – in a positive, growing way. That way the whole group is focusing its entire resources on solving problems.

- **Strong identity of group** – Remember that we mentioned the importance of gathering the church around the flag of the Mission. If you make that Mission plain and simple to understand, and if you succeed in getting everyone to sign up for it and devote themselves to that cause, the church can survive all sorts of changes along the way. The work of the church continues, even when individual members and leaders move on – because the cause continues.

- **Procedures** – What I mean by this is establishing rules by which the church approaches its functions, solves its problems, motivates people for action in the field, addresses its needs, etc. If people can fall back to a well-established habit – "this is how we do this" – the system almost runs itself. Just make sure you establish the right habits! They must be from Scripture, aimed at achieving the Mission, and yet not obstructing the church's freedom to respond to unique situations. Then a change of leadership won't compromise the Mission; in fact, the daily operations of the church will hardly be affected during the transfer.

Duplicate yourself

One reason that churches don't do well when a leader has to leave is because that person was doing everything in the church. That ought not to be; in fact, it's criminal. It denies the fact that the Lord has given many gifts to the church, and all the people in the church were called to be priests serving in the Lord's temple. There is not just one teacher in the church; you are one of several. But many leaders are so insecure that they can't let someone else work alongside them; it steals their glory, and they can't handle shared leadership and responsibilities. They feel that only they are qualified to do the job well.

You are not a one-man-show. For that matter, only the Lord Jesus himself is qualified to do everything, and even he has decided to let us help in his project. Each of us are minor players compared to him. None of us has the corner on the truth, none of us has his wisdom and power, and we are all pretty much in the same position – we can't do anything right unless the Lord enables us. So it's time to shed this pride and take on a good dose of humility. Jesus doesn't *need* any of us; he's allowing us to share in his glory by giving us a share of his glory.

So if you really care about the sheep, and if you understand that this is the Lord's project, not yours, it's time to build the church to reflect that. For example, you have to cross-train others for your job. You can't do all the teaching: so train others to take your place and teach the Word when you are not there. Train others to teach the groups in the church that you can't reach. Duplicate yourself; give them the resources that you use to teach. The military does this for a very practical reason: they don't want just one man to be trained in running the radio, for example; because if that man gets killed, the unit won't have any way of communicating – because nobody else knows how to do it.

The idea is not to make yourself indispensible, but to make the group self-sufficient – or more correctly, God-dependent. You have heard the saying that it's far better to teach a man how to fish than to give him a fish. It is, after all, the church's Mission to help each Christian reach his goal of righteousness and life with God. The Mission is *not* to make you great in the church. This is going to ensure the survival of the group, when they learn how to depend on the Lord (not you) and follow the Lord's leading in their lives even when you are not there leading them.

Avoid isolation and mutiny

Unfortunately not every church ministry job works out well. At first the new pastor and his congregation seem to be getting along well, and then something happens to sour the relationship. As time goes on, the animosity and distrust grow until the situation gets out of hand, and there's a war between the leader and the members. He can't get them to follow him, and they absolutely refuse to cooperate. A number of factors can bring about this kind of dilemma, but the result is usually ugly: either there's a church split with one party going off on its own, or the pastor himself has to leave. Either way, there's no way he can leave a peaceful legacy for the next person in line. By now the church simply won't trust any leader.

Let's assume that you are doing your best to follow the Lord's leading and you are not the real problem (although many leaders are, since not everyone in the ministry is on the Lord's side!). What should you have done to avoid this situation?

- **Distribute responsibilities** – As I mentioned before, the leader has a big red target on his chest that troublemakers naturally aim at. For some reason some people refuse to be led except in directions that please them. They have this spirit of insubordination.

> For there are many rebellious people, mere talkers and deceivers, especially those of the circumcision group. (Titus 1:10)

There is one effective way of blunting the damage that these kinds of people can do in the church: distribute the responsibilities of leading. If you are the primary worker in the church, it will be easy to find fault with you and get a party of rebels worked up against you. But if there are several elders on the team, and they are doing much of the work in the church, the rebels can't single you out of the group so easily. If a few of your elders teach, and a few of them shepherd the sheep, and a few of them lead special projects – and you are doing more coordination of efforts instead of always being out front, then troublemakers are going to have a hard time making a case that you are the source of trouble in the church.

And when trouble comes, you will have a team at your back helping to defend you and put the troublemakers in their place. A single person can't easily fight a group of people who want to take him out; but a board of elders is good insurance against it. An old Russian proverb: A stool stands best on three legs, not on one or two.

- **Deal with problems summarily** – One way to avoid an escalation of problems in the church is to address those problems as soon as they come up. Don't let them grow. When someone is making trouble, take your team of elders to him and confront him immediately with the seriousness of what he is doing. Cowards will almost always back down in the face of such decisive action. But letting that weed grow (usually out of charitable feelings – we hate to cause any distress!) is asking for trouble: it will choke out the good plants.

And make sure you follow the scriptural guidelines when you deal with problems. Follow the Lord's procedures for two reasons: *first*, they work; *second*, nobody can accuse you of trying to solve the problem in the wrong way when you are simply doing what Jesus told you to do. Use the guideline in Matthew 18. Identify your culprit and confront him firmly but forcefully as Paul describes:

> They must be silenced, because they are ruining whole households by teaching things they ought not to teach. (Titus 1:11)

Remember that you have the whole group to consider. If you try to reconcile with this rebel on his terms, the whole church will end up suffering while he's playing his games with you. It's better to remove one rebel than let him pollute the whole group.

- **The office, not the man** – Also keep in mind that you are not there to build up your own following, or your own little cult. Your aim is to get people to follow you "as I follow Christ." (1 Corinthians 11:1) Identify your cause with the Lord's cause, and back it up by teaching what the Lord taught and doing what the Lord said to do. Some people may not like it, but they can't argue with the fact that you are doing exactly what Scripture said to do. Train them to follow a God-fearing, Scripture-teaching, holy man who is building up Christ's Kingdom, no matter who is in charge at the time. Then when the time comes to hand it over to another leader, the transfer will go smoothly – as if Jesus himself was there overseeing the transfer of leadership.

These simple principles will create long-term stability that will weather problems and give the next person a healthy situation to step into.

Document the work

In order to pass on your charge to another person and not create a disaster for him, you have to plan ahead and pass on a stable, well-oiled machine that he can simply take over and keep running in the way it's already designed to work. If the thing isn't broken, he will have no need to fix anything! If it's already a winning team, he will simply proceed forward to the next victory instead of having to disassemble things and start all over.

You will do him a world of good if you document everything for him. He needs to know where you have been, why you did what you did, what condition you have brought the church to, the resources that are available to him, and where it is headed. You will be giving him the data that you had to gather yourself at the beginning of your ministry. This will save him an enormous amount of time and effort trying to figure out all this on his own. So, make it plain to him what he's inheriting from you.

- **Clear Mission statement** – Don't assume that your replacement will know about this. As I mentioned before, not everyone in the ministry has a clear idea of the goal of the church. Even the great leaders in church history sometimes seemed to have a foggy view of the Mission. This is what you raised as a banner in your group, and the next leader will need to know what keeps bringing this group of people back to church. Your members dedicated themselves to this idea; you helped them see what is worth fighting for; they are motivated to see it through. You don't want confusion in the church with the new leader and the members of the church actually working at cross-purposes, and nobody realizing why things suddenly fell apart.

- **Word-based ministry** – The ultimate foundation, of course, is the Word. If you can explain why the church works the way it does by going back to the clear teaching of the Bible, not only can the man not argue against such an authority, but it will be simple for him to pick up where you left off. He just keeps following the same "old paths" that the Lord of the church gave us all to follow.

- **A clear history** – It will help the next leader tremendously to learn about the history of the group for which he's assuming responsibility. Keep records. I don't mean that you should collect gossip. There are certain things that should not be recorded for posterity. "Love ... keeps no record of wrongs." (1 Corinthians 13:5) What I'm talking about is the state of the church when you took over, the training process, record of spiritual growth, a list of spiritual gifts and skills, the available resources, the battles fought and their outcomes, and so on. With this information, he can keep capitalizing on the strengths of the group and keep addressing its weaknesses.

- **Clarify the hierarchy** – Let the next leader know the kind of organizational structure that is in the church. To do this, however, it needed to be a well-established reality during *your* term of ministry. This is one of those things that has to be clear to everyone, and respected by everyone, over time. If there has been any question or argument as to the roles and job responsibilities along the way, the next person is going to hear all sorts of complaining and "better ideas" from the discontents who want changes to happen that will favor themselves.

Transfer of Command

EVALUATION

Every leader has successes and failures; the vital thing is to learn from them all. Analyze what happened, identify your own weaknesses and strengths, and continue building your overall skills for future assignments.

EVALUATION

During the confusion of battle, you usually don't have much time to analyze what's going on around you. You are doing your best to keep up with events, follow your strategy, and change the plan according to changing circumstances. But woe to you if you don't analyze it after it's all over! Here is where the leader *learns* – from the experience of battle. Unfortunately there are some leaders who, after a victory, celebrate and take a vacation; or after a defeat, either drop into a dark mood and withdraw, or pass it off lightly and go into the next battle using the same losing tactics.

We tend to think that our ideas and methodology are fine, because they look OK to us. But when our ideas get tested in real life, their flaws come right to the surface. When things don't work, and when we can't get our goals accomplished, then it's time to sit down and review everything and find out what is wrong with our theories. Leaders don't usually like to accept counsel or criticism; so they have to learn the hard way – through failure. At the beginning of World War I, hard-headed French leaders thought it would be an easy thing to march against the Germans in battle; but they grossly underestimated the power of a new weapon – the machine gun. Tens of thousands were mown down in the fields in a few days. One observer remarked that it was the kind of lesson "by which God teaches the law to kings." It wasn't long before the French changed their tactics.

Either way, if things went right or wrong, it will be because you did or did not strictly follow the established rules of war. They work, if you will just implement them faithfully. Go back over the entire experience, from the training and drills to the actual conflict, and study your performance.

Evaluation

Organization

Battle tests an organization. It shows how well it was trained, the weak points, the areas that the enemy especially targeted, the strong points, the merit of the strategy and the effectiveness of the tactics used. So as you do your analysis after the battle, look at the most important areas of your organization and ask these questions – because it was strength or weakness in these areas that gave you success or failure.

- **Was there a clear hierarchy?** – It's during the battle that you can see the benefits of a hierarchy in the church. I know that very few people in the church like the thought of someone "over them"; they like to think that everyone is equal and nobody is subordinate to anybody, since we "all have the mind of Christ" and we all have the same voting power. But leaders are specially trained to provide spiritual supplies, move workers to the front line, direct the group to move in unison, and study the changing circumstances to determine the necessary tactics to use during problems. The last thing they want is someone stopping the whole church in the middle of a crisis and causing trouble.

  Like it or not, we must all accept this arrangement of leaders and followers if we hope to achieve our Mission. Christ himself set it up that way, for our good and for the growth of the Kingdom. The teachers teach, the evangelists evangelize, the counselors counsel – each of us has a job to do in the organization, and we are responsible to do our own job well and let others do their jobs. Not sticking to this arrangement will cause certain ruin to the entire army. But when everyone understands the hierarchy, it's a beautiful thing to watch – an entire army working in unison, marching together, following orders, getting things done. It makes the difference between defeat and victory. So if you didn't win your battle, it may have been a simple

Evaluation

matter of someone not following orders. It's more important than you may think.

- **Did we have a decisive way of dealing with insubordination?** – This is never a pleasant task even in the army; and it's particularly unpleasant in the church. But it must be done. We can't allow people to wreck the work of the church. The Scripture is plain about this: obey your leaders; they were placed in that position of leadership for the good of the group. Grumblers and complainers, rebels and wolves, are to be dealt with severely – so that everyone in the church will realize what a serious crime it is, and how dangerous the results of their rebellion are to the Mission.

  Deserters in particular can demoralize an army. Frederick the Great told his officers to stand behind the troops and, if one of them turned to run away during a battle, put their short sword in his belly! That's harsh, but he knew that one man running in panic from the enemy will usually cause the entire line to collapse and run away.

  In one church that I know of, there was open rebellion and a few families split the church and left. Soon there were others leaving too – the morale was down, and the pastor simply allowed them to go without challenging their commitment to the church. It wasn't long before the group was reduced to a mere handful and they had to close the doors for lack of people and money. The situation may have been saved if the leadership had been forthright about shaming the cowards and encouraging the troops to stick it out.

- **Was there cross-communication up and down the chain?** – Often a battle is lost because one part of the group doesn't know what the other part is doing. It's a shameful thing, but churches are usually hotbeds of gossip, slander, lies, mis-information and confusion.

Evaluation

Small cliques will cook up stories and slander about the leaders, and the rest of the church only finds out about these troubles when it's too late to solve the problem. Elders rule from the back room in secret, and impose changes and rules on the group with nobody knowing what's coming until it happens. One person in the church thinks that someone else in the church was responsible for something, and the other person thinks otherwise. Unless there is openness and a clear system of communication throughout the church, from top to bottom and back to the top, the work of the church will be crippled at best, and at worst will become a hotbed of accusations and wars within the ranks.

- **Was there accountability?** – Along with communications and a hierarchy, the organization works well only when people understand the importance of being accountable for their actions.

The very first thing that an army recruit learns about accountability is the simple thing of responding immediately and clearly to his sergeant's orders. That "Yes, sir!" has to be loud and clear. There's an important reason for this: when an officer gives a command to a soldier, he needs to know if that soldier heard him and understood him. In battle, lives are hanging in the balance; if the man didn't hear him, he needs to know that right away so that he can make it clear to him. If that response doesn't come back right away, there may be something wrong, and the officer may need to change his plans immediately.

The purpose of accountability, then, is so that everyone will know that the job is getting done and done well. We have to hear back from someone who was given a job to do: we must get a full report, so that we can either check it off our list as done, or take measures to fix whatever problems came up. If your group doesn't understand this simple thing, you need to teach them

Evaluation

about the importance of being accountable for their actions.

Preparation

Foresight is the key to preparation: what will we need in the day of battle? It's the reason for all those drills! Now that the battle is over, ask yourself if you need to strengthen or change the kinds of preparation work in your church.

- **Was everyone trained, cross-trained?** – Battle will show up weaknesses in training. There can never be too much training and drills. Unfortunately, in the church there is hardly any training going on, even for the leaders. That's why the church today is losing just about every battle in our culture; we have no idea what is going on or how to deal with it.

    For success, we need trained and prepared troops. We must know the Word; we have to be living in holiness; we have to act as a community; we need to be fully knowledgeable about the enemy and how he works. We must know, above all else, the ways and resources of the Lord in order to fight effectively, both defensively and offensively. All this is plainly set out in Scripture for us to learn and get skilled in.

    Cross-training is also important, because troops are always getting wounded and have to leave the field. It's a shame on the leader's part if he doesn't have a teacher waiting in the wings when someone has to bow out for some reason. Will he simply let the class starve?

    And don't forget to look at yourself in this regard. By now you should have an appreciation of how much the leader is responsible for in the church. The skills and knowledge necessary to get the group through any and every circumstance is enough to make one wonder if

Evaluation

they really want to do this! Especially if someone got hurt because of your lack of skill or ignorance.

> Not many of you should presume to be teachers, my brothers, because you know that we who teach will be judged more strictly. (James 3:1)

Did you do enough planning? Did you have the resources available at the right time? Did you move the troops to the right places? Were you ready for the enemy's attack? Or did you fail simply because you didn't study the right things beforehand, and you were surprised by situations in which you had no idea how to proceed?

- **Were resources available where needed?** – Logistics is a huge part of military procedure, though most people greatly underestimate its importance. It has to do with supplies and transportation, delivered where and when needed. People can't work or fight without eating – spiritually or physically. Did all your teachers have the necessary materials to teach their students? Were the teachers themselves fed? Did the elders have the necessary spiritual resources to do their jobs of teaching, counseling, leading, etc.?

- **Did we miss any other areas?** – Like it or not, the military science covers a great many areas. You have to be good at doing many things, and you have to cover all the bases if you hope to win your battles. Consider this: if you think this is too much work, the enemy *will* take advantage of your lack of preparation, and your casual attitude about achieving the Mission. It's your job as the leader to be well-versed in all of these areas – or else suffer defeat. Remember that for military training, officers go through three years of intensive college work.

Go back and check the list, and see what you and your church may need more work in. Teaching the Word – all of it – to the beginner, the intermediate, and to the advanced students. Training elders and deacons. Seeing to the "widows and poor" in the group. Instilling discipline in the ranks – learning, crucifying sin, living a holy life in all areas, everyone faithfully carrying out their responsibilities toward each other and the church at large. A witness to the community, in many ways. Prayer – over the right issues, "in season and out of season," and with the right attitude. Dealing summarily with wolves and troublemakers in the ranks. These and many more areas come under your oversight to make a more efficient fighting force.

The actual conflict

"In this world you will have trouble." Where in the world did we get the idea that church was a peaceful garden, full of entertainments and pleasures and "celebrations", wandering around doing whatever we want and patting each other on the back for being wonderful people? That is *not* the purpose of church! *It's a training ground to get us ready for survival in a world full of trouble.* It's the only place in the world where we *can* get those necessary survival skills. Our mission is to get people out of this world, and into the next world. The problem is that there's going to be war all along the way. There will be many enemies trying to stop us on the way to the Promised Land.

If there is ever peace in your church, consider it as a golden opportunity to prepare for war. Learn your lessons well in this classroom, for the time will come when you will have to know those lessons by heart – your very survival will depend on how well you learned them. It's time to wake up and understand what's going on here.

- **Were we ready?** – Go over the details of the last battle you were in and ask this important question. Were you wasting your time in church, playing games and having

Evaluation

fun? Or were you getting ready for real enemies in the world? The Lord's lessons in the Bible are designed to equip us against the enemy, supply us with spiritual strength in the field of battle, and pull us together as an efficient fighting force. Did you use the Word like that? Now that the battle is over, can you see what you should have done, what further training that you still need, if you were to go through it again?

- **Did we implement all of our resources?** – The difference between average leaders and great leaders is the ability to utilize all of one's resources during battle, using just what is needed, when it is needed, and where it is needed to swing the battle toward victory. Relying only on the infantry, for example, and ignoring artillery or the cavalry can lead to a disaster.

    If you are doing all the teaching in the church, your church is not going to grow very well; at the very least, you will burn out trying to supply the needs of the whole group. If your sermon, every Sunday, is an evangelistic message, how will the existing converts grow spiritually in their faith? If you don't encourage others in the church to use their spiritual gifts, how will the necessary "encouragement, leadership, administration, and helping" happen when people need these things? You have to identify all the resources, have them ready, and apply them when and where they are necessary.

- **Did we pick our own ground?** – A battle is often lost because we let the enemy pick the battlefield. Christians don't seem to be very savvy in this area. Our cultural battles are usually waged on terms more advantageous to the wicked; we often don't realize that we have lost the battle before we have begun.

    For example, there was recently a Supreme Court case in which a school challenged the right of a Christian group on campus to be officially recognized by the

Evaluation

school; the group had forbidden homosexuals from holding office in their group. When they came to court, the lawyer didn't base his argument on the Bible; his arguments were around the point of the group's "beliefs." The Bible was never mentioned. So, smelling an arbitrary rule, the Justices asked the Christians what would prevent them from picking out some other special interest group and discriminating against them too – like blacks. The lawyers for the Christian group responded that they just wouldn't do that; the status of a person doesn't represent his beliefs. What a poor defense! They didn't stand on the Bible's clear statement on the issue.

> Do you not know that the wicked will not inherit the kingdom of God? Do not be deceived: Neither the sexually immoral nor idolaters nor adulterers nor male prostitutes nor homosexual offenders nor thieves nor the greedy nor drunkards nor slanderers nor swindlers will inherit the kingdom of God. (1 Corinthians 6:9-10)

If homosexuals aren't allowed into Heaven, they certainly ought not be allowed to be officers in a Christian club. In fact the club would be entirely within its rights to eliminate anybody guilty of any of these sins listed here. Blacks, however, aren't in this list – in fact, they are mentioned elsewhere in the Bible as one among many races for whom Christ died, and certainly eligible for the Church. But since the lawyer wasn't basing his argument on the Bible, his arguments sounded capricious to the Justices. I know they are afraid to take the Bible to court, but it makes instantly clear what Christianity is and why we do what we do. To be asked to operate contrary to what is taught there is obviously to violate our faith.

Evaluation

Other points to keep in mind: you can't fight a battle before you are ready. You can't let yourself be goaded into a knee-jerk reaction against people who are baiting you. You certainly don't want to be led into a trap. You don't want to be constantly dominated by the enemy, always on the defensive. You can't just accept the definitions that the enemy uses, and fight under his conditions and terms. Remember that the Lord's weapons "bring down strongholds;" so if you lost a battle, you probably gave the victory away before you started.

- **Who was involved? Who was not involved? Why?** – You may want to check your records to see if someone wasn't doing their part in the effort. There are such things as slackers in the army. Either from laziness, or apathy, or cowardice, or fear, some of your church members may be dropping out of the picture and forcing others to take up their responsibilities. Or some elder was taking a nap and nobody else could step in the gap for him. We need everyone in this effort. If every person doesn't do his or her part, the whole group suffers. This comes out painfully when the going gets rough, and someone's negligence causes others to hurt or the cause to fail.

- **Was it a classic conflict, or a unique situation?** – We can accept a loss more easily if we have prepared extensively for any kind of possibility and then get hit with something totally unexpected. It happens to the best of us. Just learn from it and be prepared the next time.

  But it's embarrassing, and to our shame, if we were hit with a simple problem and failed. How many times has sexual immorality destroyed the leadership of a church? How many times have the treasurers run away with the finances? Why do we insist on setting up churches along strictly democratic lines, accepting no leadership, and then falling under the inevitable chaos and conflict of wills? Why do we keep letting liberal theology infiltrate our ranks? By now we ought to have routine procedures and rules to avoid such disasters. If we don't, we deserve to lose.

- **Did we follow established guidelines in Scripture?** – The Lord is faithful; he will always provide us what we will need for battle before it happens. He knows what's coming. These battles are actually tests, examinations, that he uses to teach us important lessons. Nothing happens apart from his will of preparing us for the next world. The answers for all of our problems are in the Bible somewhere. The question is whether we will bother to study them before the battle, or after it's too late to use them.

  These Scriptural principles work. God specially designed them to work for all of our needs. The fault is not with the Bible's truths, the fault is that we aren't using them in the right way or we aren't using them at all. We may not understand why we have to do it God's way, but then battle is a great educator. We will learn the hard way if we are not willing to trust him and learn the easy way.

Success

Success is sweet, but it's important to learn from it. Examine what happened honestly and thoroughly and try to understand what happened – or else you may not succeed again!

- **Did we know what we were doing?** – Or did God simply get us through miraculously in spite of our ignorance? God is committed to getting his children to Heaven, one way or another. But there's such a thing as ignorantly blundering along instead of using your head. Jesus complained once that "the people of this

Evaluation

world are more shrewd in dealing with their own kind than are the people of the light." (Luke 16:8) For some reason we resist getting wiser, growing up, becoming more responsible, taking a more spiritually mature view of things. We keep forcing God to carry us like babies. Not all Christians are necessarily wise, and God often has to work around our ignorance and willfulness. Remember that God had to use a donkey once for his purposes.

And sometimes we win, though we don't realize how much God had to make up for our shortcomings to get us there. We like to take the credit for our wins. But "don't think more highly of yourself than you ought." Whatever you have is a gift from God; you are a long way from being the spiritually mature and capable warrior that he expects of you. Peter, after the resurrection, was not yet ready to serve Christ as he ought. Though he saw thousands come to Christ in his first sermon, he then showed his immaturity on at least two occasions after that.

- **Was it a long-term or short-term success?** – One fight often brings on another one. That's why we can't sit back and relax after a victory. The enemy is still prowling around out there, and he's looking for a relaxation of our defenses as a chance at a second attack.

  If you managed to talk someone out of committing suicide, for example, or getting an abortion, your job is just begun. Evidently their worldview is really warped them to consider such things. You (or someone else) are going to have to spend a lot of time educating them, disciplining them, holding their hand, supplying their needs, plugging them in somewhere in the community, etc.

  Did you manage to educate your members about the basics of the faith? Don't stop there! Paul told us that

Evaluation

a little knowledge is often more dangerous than no knowledge at all.

> The man who thinks he knows something does not yet know as he ought to know. (1 Corinthians 8:2)

Take them further into the truth, to the "deep truths of the faith," if you want them to be effective Christians.

> We have much to say about this, but it is hard to explain because you are slow to learn. In fact, though by this time you ought to be teachers, you need someone to teach you the elementary truths of God's word all over again. You need milk, not solid food! Anyone who lives on milk, being still an infant, is not acquainted with the teaching about righteousness. But solid food is for the mature, who by constant use have trained themselves to distinguish good from evil. (Hebrews 5:11-14)

- **What exactly turned the tide?** – If you won the battle, find out why. You want to remember that the next time you fight! Either you did something right, or the enemy did something wrong that you exploited. Identify it, write it down, study it, and keep it in mind for the next situation where you can use it again.

- **Will it work again, or should we fine-tune the system?** – But what works one time may not work a second time. Our enemies aren't stupid. They will study their loss, and they will be better prepared next time; they probably won't make that mistake again. If they failed to overcome your thoroughly Biblical teaching, for example, they'll do what the Midianites did to the Israelites and tempt someone in your group to fall to immorality. Don't make the mistake of thinking the battle will always be fought in the same way every

Evaluation

time. Savor the win, but prepare for a new challenge from a very vicious, creative, and persevering enemy.

Failure

A lost battle doesn't mean a lost war. General Washington lost most of his battles during the American Revolution; but through dogged persistence he kept pulling his little army together after every defeat and trying again, until they eventually won the war. So *learn* from the failure; the only real failure in war is if you do the same mistake twice!

- **Was the fault with leadership or followers?** It could have been either or both. Poor leaders will blame their followers every time for a loss in battle. But a good leader will accept the blame for his part of the loss if he deserves it. General Lee made a serious mistake at Gettysburg, and he shouldered the blame entirely; his troops simply did what he told them to do. On the other hand, Napoleon knew for a fact that several of his battles could have been magnificent victories if his subordinate generals had done what he ordered – but they didn't. You have to be clear-headed about this, just and fair. The point is not to avoid blame, but find out what went wrong so that it won't happen again. Pride will inevitably produce dissension, and everyone will want to point fingers at others as they search for a scapegoat. That will help nothing. If necessary, get a non-partisan jury together to go over the situation and make recommendations.

- **Were we blindsided?** – The key to success, as Liddell Hart says in his book on ***Strategy***, is to hit the enemy where he least expects it. And if you lost a battle, you probably were hit unawares from an unexpected direction. Why weren't you ready for that? Why didn't you have a plan to take care of it?

Evaluation

For example, one church had a music director who was being rebellious against a church policy of not using people living in open sin for ministry work. Then a board member took up her cause against the pastor and the rest of the board, and he also enlisted a church member who wasn't even on the board to help him. In just a couple of weeks the whole church was in an uproar, almost half the church left, and the rest painfully tried to put a church back together. The problem was that the church didn't have a clear policy in place, nor did it have the necessary government structure, to deal with either situation: guiding the music director in church policy, and dealing with insurrection on the board. So it easily came apart at the seams. A little foresight about putting together a Biblical church government could have prevented this disaster.

- **Does it point out weaknesses in our structure, procedures, personnel, resources?** – A failure usually means that you didn't do your homework. Well-prepared and well-supplied armies rarely lose battles. You may have to go back over the lessons to see what it was that people didn't understand. You may have to find out who isn't talking to who anymore, or who is fighting with who, and fix the weakness in the organization. You may have to question people and find out what they did (or didn't do) in the situation, and establish a clear procedure for the next time around. Do some research and look for overlapping responsibilities (that means that something didn't get done because one person thought the other person did it!). There's probably a smoking gun somewhere; for the sake of future battles, you will have to find it and fix it.

- **Which of the five pillars were missing or weak?** – Remember that we said you need all five pillars (David's plan) in your church if you want to be able to handle any situation. They are more important than you may think. Consider them as five posts that hold the roof up. Take one pillar out, and what will happen? The roof will weaken, and eventually collapse under strain. Now consider that it's a rare church that has even three of these pillars in place! No wonder that it's just a matter of time until the church will have problems that they can't solve. They don't have the necessary resources in place to solve them. It may take a while, but it will come down eventually. Failure can almost always be traced back to missing pillars.

POSTSCRIPT

This may look like a huge undertaking, this matter of leadership. There are so many things to think about, so many things to take care of. But you have to realize that the requirements of God's army are complex and wide in scope; this is actually a good view of the whole job. The secret to mastering the art of leadership isn't genius – it's the ability to break down the otherwise overwhelming job into smaller functions and steps that can then easily be solved piecemeal. From here, then, it's just a matter of methodically taking care of each part.

If it seems as if this is too much to do, if it seems unnecessary to you, then maybe you are not cut out to be a leader. There's nothing wrong with that; it's just that it's better to find that out now, before you start, instead of getting half-way through a disaster and then wanting out. Not everyone is able to handle this kind of job. In fact, the ratio should be about one to ten – a leader of some sort for every ten church families. Military leaders endure this rigorous training program; why shouldn't the Church – when so much more rests on the outcome?

On the other hand, if I haven't filled in the blanks well enough in some areas, it's for two reasons: *first*, I don't feel justified in turning this into an unwieldy book. "Short and sweet" is the best way to get students to study! *Second*, it's the leader's job to think about the principles of war – to think deeply on them. You will learn the most by turning the principles over and over in your mind, and practicing them in any and every situation. I have spent several years studying military science and thinking about how to apply it in the church setting. You will have to learn the principles and then think deeply on how to apply them to the battles that you face. It's the leader's job to contextualize the data to solve the problems in his own circumstances.

War is inherently unpredictable; but the best leaders can see the principles of warfare in whatever situation they are in. That's only because, as Napoleon taught us, they faithfully followed the established rules of warfare. There's only so much that a textbook on war can do

Postscript

for you; you must take it from here, profit from it, and win your own battles.

May the Lord be with you on the battlefield, and give you victory in his Name.

DETAILED OUTLINE

Introduction   5

The Bible and war	8
Basic principles – and being alert	8
The need for war	9
Leadership	12
War principles	13
Train, train, train	15
Time for discipline	16

The Bible and war   19

Forced into war	21
Reasons for war	22
1. Our lifeline to God	23
2. Our resources at risk	24
3. Destructive temptations	25
4. Neighbors dead and dying	26
5. Assaults of the enemy	27
The nature of our enemies – get this right!	28
▪ The heart	29
▪ The world	30
▪ Satan	31
▪ More troubles	32
Old Testament war – the model	34
New Testament war	36
Counsel about war	37
War strategies and tactics	39
The Commander	41
Leaders	43
Troops	45
The Point	47

Self-preparation   49

Self Discipline

    God-centered discipline   51
    Prayer   52
    Study   56
    Dealing with the enemy   57
    Perseverance in trouble   59

Command of the Bible   60

    The Bible is the revelation of God   61
    Themes   62
    Old Testament and New Testament   63
    Principles of Christianity, church   64
    Teaching skills   66

Learn human nature   68

    Study the heart   68
    Tap into spiritual resources   69

Learn war   70

    Assessment of situations   70
    Principles of warfare   71
    Strategies and Tactics   72
    Leadership principles & character   72
    The Lord's Mission   73
    Bible examples   73

Wider studies   74

    History   74
    Biographies   74
    Theology   75
    Heresies   75

Why the Military Model?   76

Assessment of the Position   79

Areas to examine   82

    ▪ Statement of faith   82

Detailed Outline

- Job description 83
- Hierarchy 84
- Facilities 85
- Leadership 86

Questions to ask 86

Is it good ground? *87*

- Strong lines of operation 87
- Freedom of movement 88
- Cannot be dominated 89
- Can reach all areas 90
- Communication networks 91
- Good view of enemy 92
- If not, can we easily get to good ground? ... 93

How is enemy situated? *93*

Nature of enemy influence: past, present 94
Individual and church levels 94
What are needs of group? 95
Our weapons, skill – effective? 96

Not serious problems with – *96*

- Temptations
- Sins
- Heresies
- Political correctness
- Liberalism
- Lies

Are the right resources available? *97*

Is there one commander at the top? *99*

- Are the elders supportive of my leading? ... 100
- How qualified are the leaders? 102
- What are they in charge of now? 102
- Are there isolated commands? 103
- Are there overlapping commands? 103
- Any alliances present? 104
- What would it take to fire me? 105

Can I achieve the objective? *106*

- Is it open to tactics, methods? 106
- Is everyone willing? 107
- Does everything look feasible? 107
- Will it take short or long-range strategy? 107
- How much drill and training required? 107
- Which pillars are present, which missing? 107

Assuming Command 109

The Starting Point 111

Form new teams, re-train 111
Make the Mission clear 112
Start with the basics 113
There will be resistance 114

Form Team 116

Find the willing 116
Isolate the unwilling 116
Form a method of dealing with problems 116
Implement accelerated training program 117
Have division of labor 118

- Lieutenants 119
- Engineers 119
- Logistics, supply depots 119
- Outposts 120
- Reconnaissance team 120

Communications 120

Declare the Mission 121

Create schedule 123

Organization 124
Training covered 124
Formation of ministries 124
Battles 125
Movement – depots – supply lines – fortresses 125

Detailed Outline

Reconnaissance — 126

    Demographics — 126
    Esprit of group — 127
    Issues being dealt with — 128
    Physical plant — 128
    Identify needs — 128
    Power centers — 129
    Individual talents — 129
    Individual liabilities — 130
    System flow – how things get done — 130
    Larger community context — 130
    Impediments to movement — 130

Problems to solve — 131

    Teach people who don't want to learn — *132*

- Show holes in understanding — 132
- Bring out richness in Old Testament — 133
- Test for mastery — 133
- Set up battles to win — 134
- Expose the world's true nature — 134
- Select proper materials — 135
- Connect knowledge with holiness — 135

    Lead to Heaven those who want to stay here on earth — *136*

- God-centered, Christ-centered hope — 136
- Expose temptations of world — 137
- Take heart, mind off this world — 137
- Give up goods — 137
- Focus in prayer — 138

    Make more righteous those who think themselves OK — *138*

- Plan for opposition — 139
- Be specific about sins — 139
- Tie sins to suffering, defeat — 140
- Show reasons for humility — 140
- Offer a way of escape — 141
- Train for walking with Jesus — 141

    Discipline those who won't be led — *141*

- Honor Christ as the Head — 142
- Explain discipline — 142
- Promote team spirit — 143

Detailed Outline

- Make an example of offenders, slackers — 143

Make responsible those who don't want to work — ***144***

- Expose weak links — 144
- Create community — 145
- Keep antennae up for spiritual gifts — 145
- Be specific in duties — 146
- Require accountability — 146

Key Elements to leadership — 147

- Identify program with Christianity — 147
- Base it on the Word — 147
- Do it yourself also – lead from the front — 147
- Trust the Lord's gifts — 147

Preparation and Planning — 149

The Mission — 151

There to serve — 152
Spiritual hospital — 152
Real change — 154
The five pillars — 154
Focus to win — 155
Everyone's goal — 156
Quiet times for drill, preparation — 156

Intelligence — 157

Progress reports — 157
Communication up and down the chain — 158

Fortifications — 159

Defense — 159
Stores — 160
Armor of God — 161
Backed up to the strong point — 162
Built on the Rock — 164
Engineers — 166
Encampment rules — 166

Detailed Outline

Discipline	**166**
Accountability	167
Trimming whatever doesn't belong	168
Survival skills	169
Standards	171
Drills	172
Dealing with problems	176
Logistics	**177**
Teachers	177
Everything necessary	178
Training materials	179
Training sessions	180
Depots	180
Gifts	181
Lines of operations	182
Planning	**183**
For changes	184
For coordination of efforts	184
For tiered distribution	185
For flexibility	186

War Principles — 187

Our enemies	**190**
Spiritual enemies	
• The world	190
• The flesh	190
• The devil	190
Identify the true enemy	191
Recognize dupes and traitors	192
Deal summarily with them	193
Organization	**194**
Assignments and specialties	194
Accountability	195
Command and Control	196
Assessment functions	197

Detailed Outline

Battlefield problems	**198**
Weariness	198
Protracted struggles	199
Defeats	199
Barriers from enemy	201
Friction	202
Fog	203
Shortages	206
Emotion	207
Casualties	208
Offense	**209**
Against our enemies	
• Against the world	210
• Against the flesh	212
• Against the devil	214
Offensive weapons	216
• Prayer	216
• Bible Study	218
• Fellowship	218
Offensive tactics	219
• Full combat power	219
• Seize and maintain initiative	220
• Hit the weakest point	220
• Divide and conquer	220
Defense	**221**
Reform quickly	222
Maintain standards	222
Watch for an opening	223
Movement	**224**
Spiritual growth	224
Quick response	225
Following the terrain	225
Checklist	226
Secrecy	227
Lines of operation	228
Unified responses	229

Traveling light	230
Following waypoints	231

Esprit — **232**

Alliances — **233**

Problems within — **235**

Traitors, rebels	236
Logistics	237
Movement	237
Different levels of expertise	238

Transfer of Command — 239

Stability — 242

Self-feeding group	242
Good communications	243
Strong identity of group	243
Procedures	243

Duplicate yourself — **244**

Avoid isolation and mutiny — **245**

Distribute responsibilities	245
Deal with problems summarily	246
The office, not the man	247

Document the work — **248**

Clear Mission statement	248
Word-based ministry	248
A clear history	249
Clarify the hierarchy	249

Evaluation — 251

Organization — 254

Was there a clear hierarchy?	254

Detailed Outline

Did we have a decisive way of dealing with insubordination?	255
Was there cross-communication up and down the chain?	255
Was there accountability?	256

Preparation — 257

Was everyone trained, cross-trained?	257
Were resources available where needed?	258
Did we miss any areas?	258

The actual conflict — 259

Were we ready?	259
Did we implement all of our resources?	260
Did we pick our own ground?	260
Who was involved? Who was not involved? Why?	262
Was it a classic conflict, or a unique situation?	262
Did we follow established guidelines in Scripture?	263

Success — 263

Did we know what we were doing?	263
Was it a long-term or a short-term success?	264
What exactly turned the tide?	265
Will it work again, or should we fine-tune the system?	265

Failure — 266

Was the fault with leadership or followers?	266
Were we blindsided?	266
Does it point out our weaknesses?	267
Which of five pillars were missing or weak?	267

(The following is Wesley's account of the Societies that he organized among believers in England in the late 1700's.)

THE UNITED SOCIETIES OF JOHN WESLEY'S MOVEMENT

A company of men having the form, and seeking the power of godliness, united in order to pray together, to receive the word of exhortation, and to watch over one another in love, that they may help each other to work out their salvation.

There is only one condition previously required in those who desire admission into these societies - a desire to flee from the wrath to come, to be saved from their sins. But wherever this is really fixed in the soul, it will be shown by its fruits. Therefore it is expected of all who continue within, that they should continue to evidence their desire of salvation.

God's written Word is the only rule, and the sufficient rule, both of our faith and practice. If there be any among us who observe them not, who habitually break any of them, let it be made known to him who watches over that soul as one that must give account. I will admonish him of the error of his ways. I will bear with him for a season. But if he repent not, he has no more place among us. We have delivered our own souls.

RULES OF THE BANDS

The design of the meeting is to obey that command of God, "Confess your faults one to another, and pray one for another, that ye may be healed." (James 5:16)

To this end, we intend:

- To meet once a week, at the least.

- To come punctually at the hour appointed, without some extraordinary reason.

- To begin (those of us who are present) exactly at the hour, with singing or prayer.

- To speak each of us in order, freely and plainly, the true state of our souls, with the faults we have committed in thought, word, or deed, and the temptations we have felt since our last meeting.

- To end every meeting with prayer suited to the state of each person present.

- To desire some person among us to speak his own state first, and then to ask the rest, in order, as many and as searching

Wesley's Account of his Assemblies

questions as may be, concerning their state, sins and temptations.

Some of the questions proposed to every one before he is admitted among us may be to this effect:

- Have you the forgiveness of your sins?

- Have you peace with God through our Lord Jesus Christ?

- Have you the witness of God's Spirit with your spirit that you are a child of God?

- Is the love of God shed abroad in your heart?

- Has no sin, inward or outward, dominion over you?

- Do you desire to be told of your faults?

- Do you desire to be told of all your faults, and that plain and home?

- Do you desire that every one of us should tell you, from time to time, whatsoever is in his heart concerning you?

- Consider! Do you desire we should tell you whatsoever we think, whatsoever we fear, whatsoever we hear concerning you?

- Do you desire that, in doing this, we should come as close as possible, that we should cut to the quick, and search your heart to the bottom?

- Is it your desire and design to be, on this and all other occasions, entirely open, so as to speak everything that is in your heart without exception, without disguise and without reserve?

Any of the preceding questions may be asked as often as the occasion offers; the five following at every meeting:

- What known sins have you committed since our last meeting?

- What temptations have you met with?

- How were you delivered?

- What have you thought, said, or done, of which you doubt whether it be sin or not?

- Have you nothing you desire to keep secret?

(End of Wesley's report)

Note several things in this report:

- Salvation from sin is the real issue of Christianity. And a corollary to that is the fact of corresponding fruit replacing the sinful nature. In other words, others should be able to see a change in the new Christian as he/she stops living according to the world's immorality and starts living a holy life before God.

- Membership in the church is key to living that holy life. Not only do we find encouragement and help there, but we are also forced to prove our faith by opening our hearts and lives to each other. Hypocrisy is too easy in a superficial church where nobody is held accountable. But in a church like Wesley's Societies, everyone is agreed to get busy working on their hearts so that they will be pleasing to God. Anybody who won't agree to this arrangement obviously wants to continue to live in sin and therefore has no rightful place among God's people.

Wesley understood discipline!

FURTHER RESOURCES

Books

Following are a few titles that I have benefited from greatly in my study of general military principles.

Napoleon on the Art of War, Jay Luvaas, Simon and Schuster: 1999.

Frederick the Great and the Art of War, Jay Luvaas, Da Capo Press: 1999.

Elements of Military Art and Science, Gen. H. Wager Halleck (1815-1872), Cherev House: 2006.

The Art of War, Baron de Jomini (1779-1869), trans. by Mendell & Craighill, Cherev House: 2006.

Warfighting, A. M. Gray, United States Marine Corps, US Government: 1997.

On War, Carl von Clausewitz (1780-1831), Oxford University Press: 2008.

Commanders of the Civil War, William C. Davis, Salamander Books Limited: 1990.

Strategy, B. H. Liddell Hart, Plume: 1991.

Personal Memoirs of U. S. Grant, Ulysses S. Grant (1822-1885), Cherev House: 2006.

Films

Sometimes Hollywood manages to give us a useful view of the science of warfare beyond the usual entertainment level. Films have the benefit of showing what actual battlefield conditions are like; they take you out of the classroom and into the crisis. Following are a few of the films that were helpful to me; they show military principles in action, and how leadership succeeded or failed to utilize those principles. (I am not necessarily endorsing everything in these films!)

Master and Commander

Patton

A Bridge Too Far

Glory

Gettysburg

We Were Soldiers

Black Hawk Down

U-571

NOTES

Notes

www.ingramcontent.com/pod-product-compliance
Lightning Source LLC
LaVergne TN
LVHW051824080426
835512LV00018B/2712